Read SAP PRESS online also

With booksonline we offer you online access to leading SAP experts'
knowledge. Whether you use it as a beneficial supplement or as an
alternative to the printed book – with booksonline you can:

- Access any book at any time
- Quickly look up and find what you need
- Compile your own SAP library

Your advantage as the reader of this book

Register your book on our website and obtain an exclusive and free test
access to its online version. You're convinced you like the online book?
Then you can purchase it at a preferential price!

And here's how to make use of your advantage

1. Visit www.sap-press.com
2. Click on the link for SAP PRESS booksonline
3. Enter your free trial license key
4. Test-drive your online book with full access for a limited time!

Your personal **license key** for your test
access including the preferential offer

f723-94aj-rzce-5pwm

Object Services in ABAP™

SAP® Essentials

Expert SAP knowledge for your day-to-day work

Whether you wish to expand your SAP knowledge, deepen it, or master a use case, SAP Essentials provide you with targeted expert knowledge that helps support you in your day-to-day work. To the point, detailed, and ready to use.

SAP PRESS is a joint initiative of SAP and Galileo Press. The know-how offered by SAP specialists combined with the expertise of the Galileo Press publishing house offers the reader expert books in the field. SAP PRESS features first-hand information and expert advice, and provides useful skills for professional decision-making.

SAP PRESS offers a variety of books on technical and business related topics for the SAP user. For further information, please visit our website: *www.sap-press.com.*

Horst Keller, Wolf Hagen Thümmel
Official ABAP Programming Guidelines
2009, app. 400 pp.
978-1-59229-290-5

Hermann Gahm
ABAP Performance Tuning
2009, app. 350 pp.
978-1-59229-289-9

James Wood
Object-Oriented Programming with ABAP Objects
2009, app. 350 pp.
978-1-59229-235-6

Thorsten Franz, Tobias Trapp
ABAP Objects: Application Development from Scratch
2008, app. 500 pp.
978-1-59229-211-0

Christian Assig, Aldo Hermann Fobbe, and Arno Niemietz

Object Services in ABAP™

Galileo Press

Bonn • Boston

Galileo Press is named after the Italian physicist, mathematician and philosopher Galileo Galilei (1564–1642). He is known as one of the founders of modern science and an advocate of our contemporary, heliocentric worldview. His words *Eppur se muove* (And yet it moves) have become legendary. The Galileo Press logo depicts Jupiter orbited by the four Galilean moons, which were discovered by Galileo in 1610.

Editor   Stefan Proksch
English Edition Editor   Kelly Grace Harris
Translation   Lemoine International, Inc., Salt Lake City, UT
Copyeditor   Julie McNamee
Cover Design   Jill Winitzer
Photo Credit   Masterfile/RF
Layout Design   Vera Brauner
Production Editor   Kelly O'Callaghan
Assistant Production Editor   Graham Geary
Typesetting   Publishers' Design and Production Services, Inc.
Printed and bound in Canada

ISBN 978-1-59229-339-1
© 2010 by Galileo Press Inc., Boston (MA)
1st Edition 2010
(1st German edition published 2009 by Galileo Press, Bonn, Germany)

Library of Congress Cataloging-in-Publication Data
Assig, Christian.
   [Object services in ABAP. English]
   Object services in ABAP / Christian Assig, Aldo Hermann Fobbe, Arno Niemietz.
      p. cm.
   Includes bibliographical references and index.
   ISBN-13: 978-1-59229-339-1 (alk. paper)
   ISBN-10: 1-59229-339-5 (alk. paper)
   1. ABAP Objects (Computer program language) I. Niemietz, Arno. II. Fobbe, Aldo Hermann. III. Title.
   QA76.73.A125A8813 2010
   005.1'17—dc22
                                                2009050647

Contents

5 Internal Structure and Functioning of Object Services 117

6 Useful Enhancements for Practical Use 137

Preface

In the past few years, the use of ABAP Objects as a programming language for the application development in the SAP NetWeaver environment has significantly increased. SAP has created enhancement options with object-oriented means in SAP ERP for its customers, and even the official SAP programming guidelines demand an object-oriented development approach in ABAP.

At IOT Institut für Organisations- und Technikgestaltung GmbH (Institute for Organization and Technology Design), we've successfully used ABAP Objects since 2001 to develop applications in various customer projects. For the education of students at the University of Applied Sciences of Gelsenkirchen (in the field of enterprise information systems), we've successfully relied on ABAP Objects as the programming language in the SAP environment since 2003.

Not only based on our experience in the practical and academic area are we convinced that particularly the object-oriented programming paradigm can provide new options to advance the development of business software. To effectively use the advantages of object-oriented development in large information systems, the development environments should not only provide language elements but also as many services as possible that encourage the developers to perform basic tasks, such as persistence representation or transaction control, by using these services instead of implementing own solutions. In the case of ABAP Objects, this has the additional advantages that the services belonging to the language have been further developed by SAP in the course of time and that the users of the services can benefit from these improvements and enhancements.

SAP's Object Services in ABAP currently comprise services in the areas of persistence representation, transaction control, and query/selection service. Services like these are only used frequently if their usage and functioning are clear and user-friendly. With this book, we hope to contribute to this.

The content presented in this book isn't based on a laboratory-like use of Object Services but on the experience and results gained in many years of successful use of ABAP Objects in real life. During these years, we've deployed Object Services in many cases and with great success. However, we first had to get to know Object Services with its opportunities and restrictions before we were able to use them optimally and implement meaningful enhancements.

The goal of this book is to impart our experience of the benefit and use of Object Services to other developers in the SAP NetWeaver environment. This applies all the more as we are convinced of the use of Object Services and can recommend them to all developers. Because there is no comprehensive and complete description on the use of Object Services, we want to close this gap.

During various courses at the University of Applied Sciences of Gelsenkirchen, we could verify what a clear and comprehensible description of Object Services and their use should look like. The results are reflected in this book.

We would like to thank our families and friends for their patience. We thank Stefan Proksch, our editor at Galileo Press Germany, and Kelly Grace Harris, our editor at Galileo Press USA, for the very good collaboration. Our special thanks go to all employees at IOT Institut für Organisations- und Technikgestaltung GmbH. Without their work, we would never have been able to gather all of the experience with Object Services.

Christian Assig
Aldo Hermann Fobbe
Arno Niemietz

1   Introduction

Even though object-oriented software development is continuously gaining in significance compared to the classic structured development models, the relational model based on tables and their relationships to one another still dominates the market of database systems. In consideration of the many object-oriented software developments in which relational database systems are supposed to be used, the question arises of how you can best link the actually "objectless" relational database world with the object-oriented application logic.

Relational database systems not only provide the basis for storing data in virtually all globally used information systems. The architecture of SAP systems also provides for the storage of data in a relational database system for applications that are implemented on SAP NetWeaver Application Server ABAP (SAP NetWeaver AS ABAP).

Linking the object-oriented world with the relational world is referred to as object-relational mapping. In ABAP, Object Services support the implementation of the object-relational mapping and automate many actions that you would have to implement manually for every application or that would require developing a corresponding service.

Figure 1.1 shows the three-layer architecture that has been used in all SAP systems since the implementation of SAP R/3. The three-layer architecture consists of the following three parts:

- The presentation layer that presents the user interface in SAP GUI or in a web browser
- The application layer on which one or more application servers execute the applications written in ABAP
- The database layer that enables you to permanently store data in the form of a relational database system

Object Services are available in the application layer of SAP NetWeaver AS ABAP. They support you in connecting the database layer and the application layer.

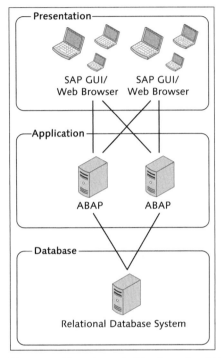

Figure 1.1 Three-Layer Architecture of an SAP System

Transient and Persistent Data

If you don't use Object Services, in ABAP — as in many other object-oriented programming languages — the objects of usual ABAP classes are designed to be edited in the same running program in which they have been created. At the latest when you end a running program, the objects of usual classes no longer exist. When you execute the program again, the objects of the usual classes from previous program calls are no longer available. You must create the possibly required objects again.

One of the main advantages of object-oriented software development is the option to map objects from the real world as software-based objects. However, objects from the real world don't only exist as long as a program runs. For mapping real objects in an information system, you need mechanisms that enable the permanent storage of objects, that is, beyond the termination of a running program.

Data that is lost when a program ends or when a computer is turned off is referred to as transient data. Persistent data, however, is stored permanently, for example, in a file or in a database. You can still access persistent data from a previous session the next time the program is started.

Object Services provide persistent classes and corresponding persistent objects so you can store objects permanently. For this purpose, Object Services then automatically write newly created or changed persistent objects to the tables of the relational database. Each program can then load the persistent objects from the database to implement further actions.

Compared to a custom implementation for object-relational mapping, the benefit of using Object Services is the considerably reduced implementation effort. Object Services have also been tried and tested for many years, so you don't need to worry about typical errors that occur in newly developed software.

Object Services also help you implement applications and entire systems on a completely object-oriented basis and fully benefit from the advantages of object-oriented development: Your software becomes more stable, and you can reuse it more often, implement it faster, and maintain it more easily than software that is developed with procedural approaches.

Contents of this Book

This book provides you with information on how you can use Object Services to develop object-oriented applications in ABAP. Object Services comprise the following three services:

▶ **Persistence Service**
The Persistence Service enables you to permanently store data from objects in the database.

▶ **Transaction Service**
The Transaction Service assists you in controlling changes made to persistent objects; i.e. in writing changes to the database and in undoing changes.

▶ **Query Service**
The Query Service provides the option to search the database for objects with specific criteria.

The individual services are designed so that they can be used with the other services. Therefore, it hardly ever happens that an application uses only one service of Object Services.

Besides Object Services, numerous additional services are available in ABAP that simplify the software development. In some of these services, SAP doesn't yet support object orientation to the extent as it would be desirable in many development projects. An example of such a service is the SAP Lock Concept. The transactions of Object Services alone are not sufficient for the consistent processing of data in systems with multiple users. The mechanism that is intended for the controlled handling of concurrent actions of multiple users — the SAP Lock Concept — contains neither object-oriented components nor object-oriented interfaces so far.

All object-oriented applications that interact with the user must also display the data from objects and enable editing. The different technologies for developing user interfaces in ABAP, however, are still supposed to display data that is formatted in the form of classic structured tables. They can't handle objects as data sources. Because of this, we also discuss how you can design the transition between object-oriented and procedural approaches without having to focus too much on the procedural approaches in your application.

Goal of This Book

This book provides you with information on how you can use Object Services to develop individual applications and entire systems with an object-oriented approach. You get detailed descriptions on the functions provided by Object Services and how these functions simplify the object-oriented software development. We also discuss how the individual functions of Object Services are implemented in the system.

You are also introduced to possible enhancements of Object Services, which you can use in any applications whose development is based on Object Services. These enhancements aren't necessarily required to use Object Services. Like Object Services themselves, they can be used frequently and considerably reduce the development work because the functions contained are implemented once at a central point. This way, you don't need to manually reimplement them in every application.

Structure of the Book

The structure of this book is based on its objective: Chapters 2 through 4 initially present the functional scope that is provided with Object Services. Chapter 5 discusses the internal structure and functioning. Chapters 6 through 8 comprise various suggestions for enhancements of the functional scope of Object Services, which are often required in practical use.

▶ **Chapter 2**, Reading Persistent Objects, introduces you to the use of the Persistence Service. You learn how to load objects from the database and how to read data from objects. Moreover, this chapter discusses how you can use existing database tables and what you should consider when modeling a new data model.

▶ After you've learned how you can read existing persistent objects from the database, **Chapter 3**, Creating and Changing Persistent Objects, describes how you can create new persistent objects and change already existing ones. For this chapter, the Transaction Service is of key importance, which supports the management of changes to persistent objects by providing an undo management function, among other things.

▶ **Chapter 4**, Selecting Persistent Objects, details the various options for selecting existing objects in the database based on given criteria. For this purpose, Object Services comprise the Query Service. However, the use of classic queries in Open SQL is also possible. Both approaches only work with objects in the database and ignore newly created and changed objects from the running program. Therefore, the last part of this chapter presents options to extend the selection to newly created and changed objects.

▶ **Chapter 5**, Internal Structure and Functioning of Object Services, describes the technological basic principles of the implementation of Object Services that facilitate the understanding of the subsequent chapters. This chapter also provides you with background information that is useful in troubleshooting or in the development of your own enhancements of Object Services.

▶ **Chapter 6**, Useful Enhancements for Practical Use, describes how you can easily enhance Object Services to facilitate their practical use. This includes simplified functions for reloading and releasing objects and the option to write data from any objects into the corresponding structures or — vice versa — to write data from the structures into the objects. You need to implement these conversions to enable the display and processing of objects in SAP user interfaces.

- Initially, persistent classes only provide functions for managing elementary data as well as individual references to other persistent objects. **Chapter 7**, Intelligent Persistent Objects, outlines how you can remove these boundaries so that you can integrate plausibility checks or store more complex data, for example all items of a sales order.

- **Chapter 8**, Integration of the SAP Lock Concept and Object Services, finally describes how you can enhance Object Services in such a way that they automate the handling of the SAP Lock Concept. You need locks whenever multiple users work with the same data at the same time. Through the integration with Object Services, you can considerably facilitate the handling of locks and at the same time design it to be more reliable than an individual implementation in every single application.

Target Audience

This book addresses readers who are involved in the software development process at different levels. Decision makers learn about the benefits of modern, object-oriented software development with Object Services in ABAP. Software architects learn how the decision to use Object Services affects the modeling of information systems. Software developers are provided with detailed information on the options provided by Object Services and how they can use them.

To fully understand the contents of this book, you should have basic knowledge of object orientation and software development in ABAP.

System Requirements

As of Release 6.10, Object Services are an integral part of every SAP NetWeaver Application Server. Object Services are also available in all systems that are based on a corresponding application server. These include, for example, SAP R/3 as of Release 4.70 and all releases of SAP ERP. This book also describes the various further developments of Object Services in subsequent releases up to Enhancement Package 2 (EhP2) for Release 7.0.

Examples and ABAP Source Code

The examples used in this book are based on SAP's flight data model that also forms the basis for most documentations, books, and trainings on the ABAP topic.

The flight data model enables the management of flights in a simplified form. This includes, for example, airports, flight plans, airlines, flight customers, and flight bookings.

It was an intentional decision to not use any examples from production software in this book. The use of the flight data model is supposed to spare you the familiarization with a complex, new data model and instead enable you to focus on Object Services. Nevertheless, the examples are selected to describe the use of Object Services in scenarios that often occur in practical use.

Because the flight data model as it's provided by SAP isn't sufficient to demonstrate all options of Object Services, the flight data model was enhanced at some points. These enhancements have the prefix /IOT/. The /IOT/ namespace is reserved for developments of IOT Institut für Organisations- und Technikgestaltung GmbH, Gelsenkirchen. The names of all classes that are not part of the standard SAP version also have the /IOT/ prefix in this book. The source code examples as well as the presented general enhancements of Object Services are within these classes. Special attention was paid to ensure that the keywords and additions to keywords were printed **bold** in all source code examples (listing) of this book. This highlighting is oriented toward the presentation of ABAP source code in the ABAP Editor to improve the legibility of listings.

The flight data model and Object Services are available in every SAP NetWeaver AS ABAP. You can download the examples and enhancements with the /IOT/ namespace that are used in this book from the publisher's website that accompanies this book (*http://www.sap-press.com*) and import them to your system.

The access to data from databases is already one of the strengths of classic ABAP. In object-oriented ABAP, Object Services in the form of persistent objects allow for an even more comfortable integration of data from databases in applications. This chapter describes how to create persistent classes and load persistent objects from the database.

2   Reading Persistent Objects

This chapter describes how you can create persistent classes and load persistent objects from the database. If you load an object from the database without using Object Services, you usually have to perform three steps:

1. Read the data from the database via an SQL query.

2. Create an object in the memory.

3. Transfer the data from the database to the newly created object.

This chapter explains how the Persistence Service of Object Services in ABAP supports you in this context.

The Persistence Service enables object-oriented access from your applications to data that is stored in the database. It automates the processes of loading objects from the database and storing objects in the database. SAP introduced the Persistence Service with the release of SAP Web Application Server 6.10. The Persistence Service has been available as an integral part in any SAP NetWeaver AS ABAP ever since. Like any other part of Object Services, the Persistence Service isn't part of the ABAP language itself. It's implemented as a service in ABAP but is still so fundamentally important that you can use it in nearly as many scenarios as the elements of a programming language.

Figure 2.1 shows a plain example of the connection between the object-oriented world in the memory and the relational world in the database. To persistently map a class, you need a database table. In Figure 2.1, this is the SPFLI database table from the flight data model. Any data record or row of this database table corresponds to an object of the class, that is, an object of the /IOT/CL_SPFLI class, in this case. You can then use a field of the database table to persistently store an attribute of the object. In Figure 2.1, the CARRID and CONNID fields are assigned to an attribute with the same name, respectively.

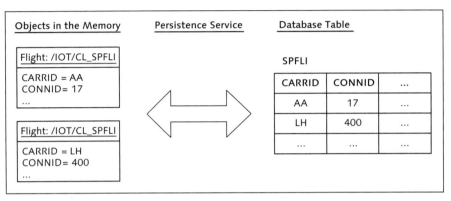

Figure 2.1 Object-Relational Mapping via the Persistence Service

This chapter describes how you can create a new persistent class and connect attributes of this class to the fields of database tables. You can then instantiate objects of the persistent class and read the values of the individual attributes. The information on persistent classes provided in this chapter enables you to create persistent classes for already-existing database tables and use class models as the basis for the creation of database tables that can be mapped to classes via the Persistence Service.

2.1   Creating a Persistent Class

You can create a persistent class like any other class, for example, using the Class Builder (Transaction SE24) or using the Object Navigator (Transaction SE80). As you can see in Figure 2.2, you simply have to select the Persistent Class class type instead of the default class type, Usual ABAP Class, when creating the class.

The system automatically creates two additional classes when creating a persistent class (see Section 5.1.1, Class Agent and Base Agent, in Chapter 5). Thus, the assignment to a package and to a transport request is prompted three times when you save a persistent class for the first time.

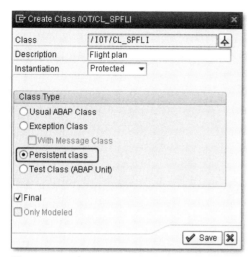

Figure 2.2 Selecting the Class Type When Creating a Class

2.1.1 Selecting a Database Table for Persistence Representation

After you create the class in the Class Builder, call the persistence representation dialog, which is only available in persistent classes, via the Persistence button or the GOTO • PERSISTENCE REPRESENTATION menu entry. You can also find the dialog for defining the persistence representation in the SAP Help Portal (*http://help.sap. com*) under *Mapping Assistant*.

If you haven't yet defined persistence representation, when you open the Persistence Representation dialog in change mode, the development environment prompts a database table or structure that forms the basis for the persistence representation. Usually, you should select a database table here. However, you might need to select a structure to store the objects on a medium other than a database. In this case, you have to implement the methods for loading and storing objects manually.

When you've selected a database table (or structure if necessary) for the persistence representation, the table and field display in the lower half of the persistence representation dialog (see Figure 2.3) lists the individual fields of the table. By selecting the database table, you define in which table the objects of the newly created class are supposed to be stored. You now have to assign each field of the table to an instance attribute of the class.

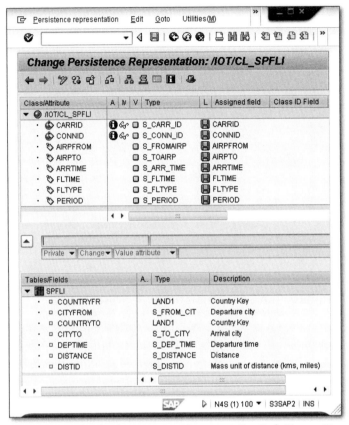

Figure 2.3 Dialog for the Persistence Representation Definition — Mapping Assistant

2.1.2 Assigning the Individual Fields to the Attributes of the Class

To assign a field to an instance attribute of the open class, select a field in the table and field display of the persistence representation dialog by double-clicking on it. Figure 2.4 shows an enlargement of the area between the tree displays of the table with its fields and of the class with its attributes. This area is referred to as the *Editing Area* in the SAP Help Portal. It enables you to configure the potential settings for the assignment of a field to an attribute.

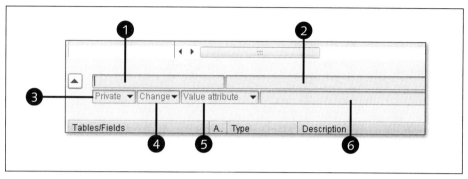

Figure 2.4 Settings for the Assignment of a Field to an Attribute

▶ **Name**

In the first input field of the upper line (❶) you can enter the name of the attribute to which the field will be assigned. The system automatically proposes the name of the selected field from the database table. In most cases, it makes sense to accept this proposal because this makes it considerably easier to track the defined representation.

Note: Maximum Length of Attribute Names in Persistent Classes

The name of an attribute of a persistent class can consist of a maximum of 26 characters. For method names in all classes and attribute names in usual ABAP classes, 30 characters are allowed.

In persistent classes, the system automatically generates at least one method for each attribute. The name of this method consists of the GET_ prefix and the name of the attribute. This method enables you to read the current value of the attribute. Because the GET_ prefix in the name of this method requires 4 characters, 26 characters remain for the attribute name.

Note: No Attribute Names that Begin with GET_ or SET_

ABAP doesn't allow the same name to be used for an attribute and a method in a class. Because the Persistence Service creates access methods with the GET_<attribute name> and SET_<attribute name> names for most of the attributes, a naming conflict between the name of an attribute and the name of a method can occur.

Consequently, you can't, for example, create an attribute named TYPE and an attribute named SET_TYPE in the same persistent class: For the attribute named TYPE, the Persistence Service creates an access method named SET_TYPE. This method name collides with the name of the attribute, SET_TYPE, which leads to a syntax error when the class is checked.

▶ **Description**
In the second input field of the upper line (❷), you can enter the description for the attribute. Here, the system proposes the description of the selected field.

▶ **Visibility**
In the first list box of the lower line (❸), you can select the visibility of the methods for accessing the attribute. Components of a class with the Public visibility setting can be accessed from any class. The Protected visibility setting limits the access to the class itself and its subclasses. Components with the Private visibility setting are available in the class only.

With one exception, the selected visibility also applies to the attribute. In persistent classes, an attribute never adopts the Public visibility. If you select the Public visibility, the methods for accessing the attribute are assigned Public visibility; the attribute itself, however, adopts a more restrictive visibility, namely, Protected. This ensures that the objects of other classes don't directly access the attribute. Instead, they use the methods provided for this purpose.

▶ **Changeability**
The second list box of the lower line (❹) enables you to specify whether the value of the attribute can be changed from any class (Changeable) or whether this can be done only in the class itself and its subclasses (Read Only). For fields that belong to a primary key of a database table, only Read access is allowed.

▶ **Assignment type**
The assignment type has the most complex setting options with far reaching effect. You select the assignment type in the third list box of the lower line (❺). Basically, the following assignments types are available:

▶ The Value Attribute assignment type is assigned to usual attributes in which you can store any property of an object.

▶ Fields with the Business Key and GUID assignment types can be used as keys for objects of persistent classes. Section 2.1.4, Instance GUIDs and Business Keys, introduces the different possible key types.

▶ The Object Reference and Class Identifier assignment types refer to fields that are used to persistently store a reference to another object. Section 2.4, Persistent References, describes persistent references in more detail.

▶ A field that has been assigned to the Type Identifier assignment type contains information on the class to which an object belongs. This assignment type is only required in persistent classes for which persistent subclasses exist. Section 2.5, Inheritance, which discusses the inheritance between persistent classes, provides more information on the functioning of the type identifier.

Table 2.1 provides an overview of the properties that a field must have to be assigned to an attribute with a specific assignment type. For example, a field that you want to assign to an attribute with the GUID, Object Reference, Class Identifier, or Type Identifier assignment type must be of the OS_GUID type. SAP uses the OS abbreviation in names of data elements, classes, and other repository objects to indicate that they belong to Object Services. One of the prerequisites for all assignment types is that the field in the database table is defined via a data element. You can't assign fields of a database table that are directly defined via a predefined type to a persistent class.

Assignment Type	Type of the Field	Key Field in Database
BUSINESS KEY	Not OS_GUID	Yes
GUID	OS_GUID	Any
VALUE ATTRIBUTE	Any	No
OBJECT REFERENCE	OS_GUID	No
CLASS IDENTIFIER	OS_GUID	No
TYPE IDENTIFIER	OS_GUID	No

Table 2.1 Assignment Types for the Persistence Representation

Fields that you want to assign with the Business Key assignment type must additionally be defined as a Key Field in the database table. If you use the Value Attribute, Object Reference, Class Identifier, and Type Identifier assignment types, the field that is supposed to be assigned can't belong to the key of the table. Section 2.1.4, Instance GUIDs and Business Keys, describes the various cases in which you can use the GUID assignment type for key fields and fields that don't belong to the key.

▶ **Attribute type**
The last input field (❻), the attribute type, enables you to define for persistent references (see Section 2.4) which objects can be referenced by specifying the name of a class or of an interface. For all other assignment types, you can't change the attribute type or the type specified doesn't have any effect.

After you've configured all settings for a field, you can use the arrow button to assign the field. The system then automatically selects the next field that hasn't been assigned yet. Assign all other fields of the selected table to an attribute in the same way before saving the persistence representation and exiting the dialog.

Particularly if the assigned database table doesn't contain fields of the OS_GUID type, meaningful values have already been configured for all settings, which makes the assignment easy. If necessary, you can retroactively change all settings without much effort. You may have to delete a field assignment first before you can reassign the field.

2.1.3   Completeness of the Persistence Representation

When you assign a database table to a persistent class in the persistence representation, it's generally necessary that you assign each field of the database table to an attribute of the persistent class. If the representation is incomplete, you can't activate the persistent class.

The Data Dictionary also enables you to extend the definition of a database after you create and activate a persistent class, for example, by adding new fields or an append structure to the database. After such a modification, you can't activate a new version of the persistent class until you have assigned all new fields in the persistence representation. The previously activated version, however, still doesn't contain syntax errors and remains active so that your programs can continue to use it. If the persistence representation is incomplete, you can't access the new fields. Note that the additional fields are empty when you create or modify a persistent object, even if they have been filled otherwise previously.

2.1.4   Instance GUIDs and Business Keys

As part of the persistence representation, you have to define a unique key by which a persistent object of the class can be identified. This key is comparable to the primary key of a database table by which a data record can be identified uniquely.

The Persistence Service distinguishes between two types of keys: the instance GUID and the business key. The instance GUID is a Globally Unique Identifier that the system assigns automatically when you create a new persistent object. The instance GUID always consists of a field of the OS_GUID type. If you want to assign the keys for objects of a persistent class manually or using a different mechanism, such as a number range object, you have to use a business key. You can use any number of fields of any type that together uniquely identify an object of a class as business keys. The only type that you're not allowed to use in a business key is the OS_GUID type.

Excursus: Globally Unique Identifiers

A number with a length of 16 bytes or 128 bits that can be used as a unique key of any object worldwide is referred to as Globally Unique Identifier (GUID) or Universally Unique Identifier (UUID). Due to the length of the key, 2128 (about 3.4 × 1038) possible values are available. Various mathematic procedures enable you to create a key that is definitely unique without having to manage the set of already assigned keys or coordinate with other systems.

In ABAP, you can generate a GUID by calling the SYSTEM_UUID_CREATE function module. As of Enhancement Package 2 (EhP2) for Release 7.0, you should use the CL_SYSTEM_UUID class to generate GUIDs. Compared to alternative concepts, for example, number ranges, the generation of GUIDs is considerably faster and less time-consuming because no communication is required between the application servers or between the application server and the database system to obtain a unique key.

Even though GUIDs provide numerous benefits for automatic processing, you always face the problem that a sequence of 32 hexadecimal numbers is definitely too much to be read or even remembered and reentered by humans. You should therefore use GUIDs for program-internal use only and shouldn't display them in user interfaces.

You can use an instance GUID, a business key, or a combination of business key and instance GUID in a persistent class. If you use only one key type, that is, either an instance GUID or a business key, this key must also be the primary key of the assigned database table, respectively. If you use a combination of instance GUID and business key, the business key must be the primary key of the database table while the instance GUID is stored in another field of the same database table.

If you use an instance GUID, you don't have to assign the key manually or via a number range object. The Persistence Service can efficiently assign the instance GUIDs locally because this can be implemented without any communication with the database system or other application servers. Because a GUID itself is already definitely unique, it isn't necessary for header-item relationships to use complex keys that are a combination of various fields, for instance. The use of an instance GUID is also a prerequisite for using persistent references (see Section 2.4).

However, instance GUIDs aren't suitable for direct use by the user. The Persistence Service consequently manages instance GUIDs automatically almost invisibly to you. Instance GUIDs are also not supposed to contain further information in addition to the identification of an object. Business keys, in contrast, can contain the creation date of an object or enable you to read the order of the created objects from multiple business keys, for example. If you use an instance GUID, you require further attributes that may include this information.

In addition to better legibility and the option to derive further information, the business key has the advantage that you can also use it when you want to access an already existing database table without instance GUID in the primary key. However, it usually involves more effort to assign a key for business keys at runtime, and you first have to consider what an appropriate business key could look like for new tables.

With a combination of instance GUID and business key, you can benefit from the advantages of both key types, but you also have to cope with the disadvantages of both types. The combination can be used in tables that don't contain an instance GUID because it's usually easier to add an additional field than to change the primary key of the database table. You benefit from the legibility of the business key and can also use persistent references. However, the assignment of the business key still involves a great deal of effort, and you may have to define an appropriate business key first. Because any persistent object contains two unique keys if you use the combination of instance GUID and business key, the memory requirement of the application server and database system increases slightly.

The Persistence Service can't map database tables with a field of the OS_GUID type and additional fields in the primary key. Due to the worldwide uniqueness of GUIDs, it doesn't necessarily make sense to add further fields to a primary key that already contains a GUID. If you still want to map this kind of constellation, instead of OS_GUID, you can use another data element with the same domain for the type of the field in the primary key, for example, SYSUUID_X. The system then doesn't interpret the field as an instance GUID, but as a part of the business key.

2.1.5 Multiple-Table Mapping

Instead of mapping all attributes of a class to a database table, you can also use the Persistence Service to define a mapping to multiple database tables, so-called multiple-table mapping. When reading and writing objects, the Persistence Service then automatically accesses several database tables.

In the persistence representation, you can add additional database tables by right-clicking on the Tables/Fields column header. The context menu, which is hidden at a rather uncommon position, solely contains the Add Table/Structure entry (see Figure 2.5). After you have selected an additional database table, you can assign the fields to the attributes in the same way as for the first database table. As of the release of EhP2 for Release 7.0 of SAP NetWeaver AS ABAP, the persistence representation dialog provides an additional button that also allows you to add another database table to the persistence representation.

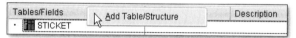

Figure 2.5 Adding Another Database Table to the Persistence Representation

Compared to multiple-table mapping, the mapping of objects of a class to a single database table usually leads to less database load and reduced access times. However, multiple-table mapping can be useful if you want to access multiple already-existing database tables via a single persistent class. Multiple-table mapping can also be used in the context of an inheritance hierarchy, which is described in Section 2.5, Inheritance.

To map a persistent class to several database tables, all database tables must use the same primary key, which means they must have the same number of key fields and the key fields have to be defined by the same data elements. Using compatible data elements, for example, with the same domain isn't sufficient. The field names and the field order within the primary key can vary between the database tables. However, for deviating field names, you have to manually change the attribute name for the persistence representation to assign the fields from the various database tables to the same attribute. If you work with a combination of business key and instance GUID to identify the objects of a persistent class, every database table has to contain the business key as the primary key and the instance GUID as an additional field.

2.1.6 Transient Attributes

In addition to persistent attributes to which you have assigned a field of a database table in the persistence representation, a persistent class can include further attributes that the Persistence Service doesn't automatically store in the database. These attributes are called transient attributes. Like attributes of usual classes, you create transient attributes in the class itself and not in the persistence representation.

2.1.7 Activating the Persistent Class

After you have created the persistent class and defined the persistence representation, you should activate all inactive repository objects. When activating a persistent class, the system may ask you if the so-called class agent is also supposed to be activated. Because you can neither create new persistent objects nor load already existing persistent objects without an activated class agent, you should also activate the class agent. The next section deals with the class agent and its tasks.

2.2 Instantiating Persistent Objects

After you have created a persistent class as described in Section 2.1, Creating a Persistent Class, you can use all basic functions of Object Services. Without you having to write a single line of ABAP source code, the Persistence Service generates classes and the corresponding methods that enable you to load persistent objects, create persistent objects, read and modify their attributes, and finally write the implemented changes to the database.

In this context, an object of the persistent class represents an object of the real world that you want to manage in your system through the Persistence Service. Such a persistent object initially merely contains the attributes that you have assigned to the individual fields of the database table as well as the access methods for reading and modifying these attributes.

The class agent of the persistent class manages all objects of a persistent class that are known in the running program. The class agent is an object of a class that the Persistence Service creates automatically when creating the persistent class. The Persistence Service derives its name from the name of the persistent class. It simply replaces CL, which refers to class in the name of the persistent class, with CA, which refers to the class agent. Consequently, the class agent for the persistent class, /IOT/CL_SPFLI, is called /IOT/CA_SPFLI.

A running program never contains more than one class agent for a persistent class. The class agents are thus implemented according to the singleton design pattern. This mechanism ensures that you can't generate additional instances of a class agent manually. Instead, the system creates exactly one instance of the class agent when accessing a class agent class in a running program for the first time. From then on, this instance manages all persistent objects of the class that are used in the running program. You can access this instance via the reference that is stored in the class agent class in the static attribute named AGENT. You can access the class agent for the persistent class, /IOT/CL_SPFLI, for example, via the /iot/ca_spfli=>agent expression.

Depending on whether the mapping in the persistence representation of a persistent class is defined via a business key, via an instance GUID, or via a combination of both, a class agent provides up to three different methods for instantiating a single persistent object. Each of the methods expects a key that uniquely identifies a persistent object as an importing parameter. As return parameters, each instantiation method provides a reference to the instantiated persistent object.

The following sections explains how you can use these methods.

2.2.1   IF_OS_CA_PERSISTENCY~GET_PERSISTENT_BY_OID

In classes in which an instance GUID is defined in their persistence representation, you can use the IF_OS_CA_PERSISTENCY~GET_PERSISTENT_BY_OID method to instantiate a single persistent object via a known instance GUID. Listing 2.1 shows how this method is called for the instantiation of an invoice object from the flight data model.

```
DATA: rf_ca_snvoice  TYPE REF TO /iot/ca_snvoice,
      rf_snvoice     TYPE REF TO /iot/cl_snvoice,
      v_guid         TYPE os_guid.

rf_ca_snvoice = /iot/ca_snvoice=>agent.

v_guid = 'D11C8049D41ACE19E1000000AC100887'.

rf_snvoice ?=
  rf_ca_snvoice->if_os_ca_persistency~get_persistent_by_oid(
    v_guid ).
```

Listing 2.1 Instantiating a Persistent Object via the Instance GUID

Listing 2.1 contains three variables: a reference to the class agent of the persistent class, a reference to an object of the persistent class, and a byte sequence that is used to store the instance GUID of the object that is supposed to be instantiated.

The first statement after the declaration of the variable assigns the respective reference variable the reference to the class agent that is contained in the static attribute (`AGENT`) of the `/IOT/CA_SNVOICE` class. The instance GUID of the object that is supposed to be instantiated is then stored in the `v_guid` variable. Here, the instance GUID or business key of the object that is supposed to be instantiated is already known in the examples. Chapter 4, Selecting Persistent Objects, discusses the options that Object Services provide to instantiate objects without an already known unique key.

Finally, the `IF_OS_CA_PERSISTENCY~GET_PERSISTENT_BY_OID` method of the class agent is called, which instantiates the persistent object. The instance GUID of the persistent object that is supposed to be instantiated is transferred to the method. If a persistent object exists for the transferred instance GUID, the method returns a reference to the persistent object.

Because the parameter interface of this method is centrally defined in the `IF_OS_CA_PERSISTENCY` interface for all persistent classes, the reference type of the return parameter is kept as general as possible by using `OBJECT`. To store the returned reference in the `rf_snvoice` variable with the more specific `/IOT/CA_SNVOICE` reference type, Listing 2.1 uses the casting operator (?=) so that a so-called downcast is implemented. A *downcast* is an assignment where a reference to an object is assigned to a variable that has a more specific type than the variable in which the assigned reference was originally stored.

Instead of using the `rf_snvoice` variable, you can also call the method with the `/iot/ca_snvoice=>agent` expression via the static attribute. However, the resulting expression is significantly longer and therefore more difficult to read. Also, an activated limitation to 72 characters per line of ABAP source code can make a call impossible in some cases when the static attribute is used directly.

Excursus: Methods defined in Interfaces in ABAP

If you use a method in ABAP in a class and the method is defined in an interface, the method is assigned a new name. This name consists of the name of the interface, a tilde (~), and the method name as it's defined in the interface. For the `IF_OS_CA_PERSISTENCY~GET_PERSISTENT_BY_OID` method, `IF_OS_CA_PERSISTENCY` is the name of the interface in which the `GET_PERSISTENT_BY_OID` method is defined.

2.2.2 IF_OS_CA_PERSISTENCY~GET_PERSISTENT_BY_KEY

If a business key is defined in the persistence representation, the IF_OS_CA_PERSISTENCY~GET_PERSISTENT_BY_KEY method provides the option to instantiate a single persistent object. Instead of the instance GUID, you have to transfer a structure to this method. The structure must contain a field with the same data type for any attribute that is a part of the business key. Here, the reference type of the result is also OBJECT, which means that you normally have to use the casting operator (?=). Listing 2.2 shows the instantiation of a persistent flight object via the IF_OS_CA_PERSISTENCY~GET_PERSISTENT_BY_KEY method.

```
DATA: rf_ca_spfli            TYPE REF TO /iot/ca_spfli,
      rf_spfli               TYPE REF TO /iot/cl_spfli,
      st_business_key_spfli TYPE scol_connection_key.

rf_ca_spfli = /iot/ca_spfli=>agent.

st_business_key_spfli-carrid = 'AA'.
st_business_key_spfli-connid = 17.

rf_spfli ?=
  rf_ca_spfli->if_os_ca_persistency~get_persistent_by_key(
    st_business_key_spfli ).
```

Listing 2.2 Instantiating a Persistent Object via the Business Key (IF_OS_CA_PERSISTENCY~GET_PERSISTENT_BY_KEY)

Warning: Order of the Fields of the Business Key Structure

If the business key for a persistent class consists of multiple fields, the order of the fields in the database table isn't the determining factor for the required order of the fields in the business key structure. In the business key structure that you pass to the IF_OS_CA_PERSISTENCY~GET_PERSISTENT_BY_KEY method, the fields of the names of the assigned attributes need to be sorted alphabetically.

As of EhP2 for Release 7.0 of SAP NetWeaver AS ABAP, you can configure the order of the fields of the business key. In addition to alphabetically sorting the names of the fields, you can then also work with the order that you used for assigning the fields in the persistence representation.

The system doesn't explicitly check if you actually stick to this order when calling the method. If you don't follow the order, you risk that the method doesn't find an existing object or returns a different object than expected.

The sample code from Listing 2.2 enables you to instantiate flight plans because the fields in the SCOL_CONNECTION_KEY structure type happen to be sorted alphabetically. But if you instantiate a persistent object for the SBOOK table in the flight data model (flight bookings), you can't use the SCOL_FLIGHT_BOOKING_KEY_S structure type because its fields aren't sorted alphabetically.

2.2.3 GET_PERSISTENT

The GET_PERSISTENT method is also available if a business key is defined in the persistence representation. This means that you can generally use the method in the same cases as the previously described method, IF_OS_CA_PERSISTENCY~GET_PERSISTENT_BY_KEY.

The parameter interface of the GET_PERSISTENT method isn't centrally defined in an interface. Using the data from the persistence representation, the Persistence Service automatically generates a parameter interface that meets the requirements of the respective persistent class. Here, the Persistence Service creates an importing parameter for any attribute that belongs to the business key, so the problem of the correct order of the fields of a structure type isn't relevant for this method.

The reference type of the return value is the persistent class to which the class agent belongs. Consequently, you usually don't have to implement a downcast with the casting operator (?=) if you use this method.

In Listing 2.3, the same flight plan object as in Listing 2.2 is instantiated with the GET_PERSISTENT method. For this purpose, the I_CARRID and I_CONNID parameters transfer the individual parts of the business key to the method.

```
DATA: rf_ca_spfli TYPE REF TO /iot/ca_spfli,
      rf_spfli    TYPE REF TO /iot/cl_spfli.

rf_ca_spfli = /iot/ca_spfli=>agent.

rf_spfli =
  rf_ca_spfli->get_persistent(
    i_carrid = 'AA'
    i_connid = 17 ).
```

Listing 2.3 Instantiating a Persistent Object via the Business Key (GET_PERSISTENT)

2.2.4 Exception Handling

Object Services always use class-based exceptions, which were introduced with SAP NetWeaver AS Release 6.10. If one of the methods described is executed for instantiating a persistent object, an exception of the CX_OS_OBJECT_NOT_FOUND class can occur. The exception always occurs if you pass a key in the form of an instance GUID or a business key for which no persistent object exists in the system to the method. While these methods are executed, the Persistence Service checks if an object with the passed key is stored in the assigned database table and if a new persistent object with the passed key has been created within the running program.

The management state of a persistent object (see Section 3.4, Management States of Persistent Objects, in Chapter 3) can also raise an exception of the CX_OS_OBJECT_NOT_FOUND class: The three methods for the instantiation of persistent objects return neither deleted nor transient objects; instead, they also raise an exception of the CX_OS_OBJECT_NOT_FOUND class in these cases.

Exceptions of the CX_OS_OBJECT_NOT_FOUND class belong to the CX_DYNAMIC_CHECK category, so you should always catch and handle these exceptions in a reasonable manner — as shown in Listing 2.4 — if you can't rule out this kind of exception. But if you've ensured that the requested persistent object actually exists, for example, by already having created it in the running program previously, you don't have to catch the exception.

```
DATA: rf_ca_spfli          TYPE REF TO /iot/ca_spfli,
      rf_spfli             TYPE REF TO /iot/cl_spfli.

rf_ca_spfli = /iot/ca_spfli=>agent.

TRY.
    rf_spfli =
      rf_ca_spfli->get_persistent(
        i_carrid = 'AA'
        i_connid = 17 ).
    CATCH cx_os_object_not_found.
*      Exception handling
       ...
ENDTRY.
```

Listing 2.4 Instantiating a Persistent Object Including Exception Handling

An exception of the CX_OS_NO_IMPLEMENTATION class occurs when you call a method that the Persistence Service has not generated for this persistent class due to the settings in the persistence representation. This is always the case if no instance GUID is defined and you call the IF_OS_CA_PERSISTENCY~GET_PER-SISTENT_BY_OID method, or if no business key is defined and you call the IF_OS_CA_PERSISTENCY~GET_PERSISTENT_BY_KEY method. The exceptions of the CX_OS_NO_IMPLEMENTATION class belong to the CX_NO_CHECK category. Usually, you aren't supposed to catch exceptions of this category. If this kind of exception occurs, it's a valuable tip for your search for the cause of an error in a program.

The GET_PERSISTENT method doesn't exist in the class agent if no business key is defined in the persistence representation. Consequently, an exception of the CX_OS_NO_IMPLEMENTATION class is never raised.

> **Note: Exceptions of the CX_OS_CLASS_NOT_FOUND Class**
>
> In the two methods from the IF_OS_CA_PERSISTENCY interface, the CX_OS_CLASS_NOT_FOUND exception class is additionally declared. However, we've never come across a constellation in which an exception of this kind is actually raised by these methods — neither in the SAP documentation nor in the source code of the Persistence Service.

2.2.5 Behavior for Already-Loaded Objects

All methods of the class agent for the instantiation of persistent objects check if the requested object already exists in the management of the class agent before accessing the database. If the requested object is already known and loaded, the corresponding method simply returns a reference to the existing object without accessing the database.

Compared to database accesses with an SQL statement in structured programming, a major advantage is that the Persistence Service ensures that the same instance of the same object is always used within one internal session. The risk of unintentionally working with several copies of the same data and modifying some of the copies of the data without noticing it isn't given if you always use the Persistence Service. This eliminates a potential source of inconsistencies, additional data load issues, and additional memory consumption issues, which means the behavior of the Persistence Service also ensures that applications run faster.

However, you should note that calling an instantiation method doesn't always automatically indicate the current state of the database. You have to request this kind of update for an already-instantiated object explicitly if necessary. Chapter 3, Section 3.4, Management States of Persistent Objects, introduces the options available for updating persistent objects.

2.3   Reading Attribute Values

The individual attributes of a persistent object are accessed via instance methods of the persistent class whose names respectively consist of the GET_ prefix and the name of an attribute. Each of these methods has only one parameter, namely, a return value that the method uses to return the value or reference stored in the attribute. Listing 2.5 shows how you can read the value of attributes of a persistent flight plan model that has been instantiated previously in the same way as shown in Listing 2.3.

```
DATA: rf_spfli   TYPE REF TO /iot/cl_spfli,
      v_distance TYPE s_distance.

* Instantiate the persistent flight plan object
...

* Read the distance attribute (DISTANCE)
v_distance = rf_spfli->get_distance( ).
```

Listing 2.5 Reading the Value of an Attribute of the Persistent Object

When using Object Services, it's possible for various reasons that an instance of a persistent object exists in the memory of a running program, but the attributes haven't been filled yet. This kind of object is also referred to as a *representative object* for a persistent object in the SAP Help Portal. For a representative object, the Persistence Service automatically reads the values of the attributes from the database as soon as they are required, for example, when there's an attempt to read the value of an attribute via a GET method. This behavior corresponds to the *lazy loading* design pattern.

If the reloading of the attributes' values fails because the database doesn't contain an object for the given key, a GET method raises an exception of the CX_OS_OBJECT_ NOT_FOUND class. In many cases, you can avoid this exception already during the development time, for example, by explicitly instantiating the persistent object in advance or calling other GET methods. For GET methods, it's therefore usually neither useful nor necessary to catch exceptions of this class. Chapter 3, Section 3.4, Management States of Persistent Objects, which discusses transitions between management states of persistent objects, helps you determine if a persistent object in your program might exist as a representative object in the memory.

If you use persistent objects, you have to consider the object-oriented data encapsulation concept because every attribute of a persistent class is assigned the Private or Protected visibility. This way the Persistence Service prevents direct access to the attributes of a persistent object outside the persistent class and its subclasses.

In the methods of the persistent classes, subclasses, and class agent, direct access to attributes is technically possible. However, direct read access to attributes of persistent classes isn't recommended. This access contradicts the object-oriented data encapsulation concept. For persistent objects, this can also result in deactivating the mechanism for automatically reloading an object that has not been loaded yet.

Excursus: Data Encapsulation

Data encapsulation is one of the basic concepts of object-oriented software development. The concept allows you to access the attributes of an object only in the class itself. From all other positions, you have to read or set the values of individual attributes by calling the corresponding method. Typically, the names of methods for reading a value begin with GET, methods for writing a value begin with SET.

This way, you can prevent direct access to individual attributes that violates dependencies between the attributes. The calling program of a method doesn't have to know anything about how the data is stored internally.

If you've assigned a field as the instance GUID in the persistence representation, you can't access the value directly via a GET method of the persistent class because the instance GUID is available in the Persistence Service for internal use only. If you do need to access the instance GUID of a persistent object, however, you can determine it via the IF_OS_CA_SERVICE~GET_OID_BY_REF method of the class agent. The method expects as an importing parameter a reference to the persistent object for which it's supposed to determine the instance GUID for.

2.4   Persistent References

Usual references are only valid during the runtime of a program. This behavior is similar to the behavior of objects of usual classes: They only exist as long as a program runs. Because the references refer to the addresses in the memory of the running program, they can't be stored in the database like an attribute of an elementary type. After persistent references of the Persistence Service have been set, they are stored in the database just like any other attribute of a persistent object so they are also available when the same program or another program is executed the next time without having to be set again by the application.

Instead of a reference to an address in the memory, the Persistence Service stores two pieces of information in the database: to which class the referenced object belongs and which object of this class has been referenced. Accordingly, a database table that is supposed to contain a persistent reference for each object or row must include a field for the class GUID and a field for the instance GUID. The two fields for mapping a persistent reference must be of the OS_GUID type. You don't have to create additional data types to reference an object of a specific class.

You can use persistent references only to reference a persistent object in another persistent object. The referenced object can also belong to a different class than the referencing object. Because the referenced object is identified by the instance GUID, an instance GUID needs to be defined in the persistence representation of the class of the referenced object. Class GUIDs are available for all classes because the system creates them automatically for each ABAP class. The assignment between the class name and class GUID is implemented with the SEOCLASS database table.

Figure 2.6 provides an example of the values of a persistent reference in the memory and in the database. This is based on a different variant of the flight data model where the database table with the sales counters contains two additional fields of the OS_GUID type. These fields are used to reference the airport where the sales counter is located. Compared to the SAP flight data model, every airport is additionally provided with an instance GUID.

The Lufthansa sales counter with counter number 1 is located at Frankfurt Airport. Therefore, the corresponding counter object contains a reference to Frankfurt Airport. The Persistence Service stores this information in the AIRPORT_CLASS and AIRPORT_INSTANCE fields of the counter table in the database. The F904... class GUID and SEOCLASS table provide the information that an airport is referenced. The 6C71... instance GUID indicates which airport is referenced.

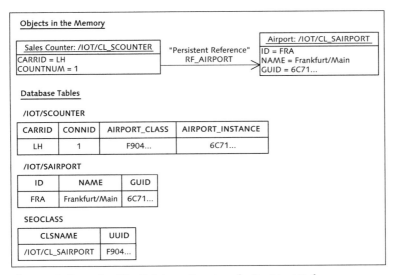

Figure 2.6 Example of the Database Mapping of a Persistent Reference

2.4.1 Definition of a Persistent Reference in the Persistence Representation

To create a persistent reference, you have to assign the two fields of the database table with the class GUID and the instance GUID to an attribute of the class in the persistence representation of the persistent class that is supposed to contain the persistent reference. Assign the field with the class GUID using the Class Identifier assignment type (see Figure 2.7), and assign the field with the instance GUID using the Object Reference assignment type (see Figure 2.8). It's important to change the name of the attribute manually in this case: To assign both fields to the same attribute, you must specify the same attribute name when assigning the two fields (here: RF_AIRPORT).

Figure 2.7 Assigning the Field with the Class GUID in the Persistence Representation

Figure 2.8 Assigning the Field with the Instance GUID in the Persistence Representation

For a plain reference variable, the reference type limits the objects that you can assign to the variable. For persistent attributes, the attribute type (in Figures 2.7 and 2.8 /IOT/CL_SAIRPORT, respectively) determines which objects you can reference with the persistent reference:

▸ In the simplest case, you specify the concrete class to which all referenced objects will belong directly.

▸ If all referenced objects belong to a shared superclass, you can define the superclass as an attribute type.

▸ If all referenced objects implement a specific interface, this interface could be used as the attribute type.

▸ If you want to reference persistent objects of all types without limiting the type, you should use the OBJECT attribute type. The Persistence Service also uses the OBJECT attribute type if you don't specify the attribute type explicitly.

You can use the access methods (see Section 2.3, Reading Attribute Values, in this chapter, and see Section 3.2, Changing Attribute Values, in Chapter 3) to access the defined attributes with a reference type in the same way as attributes of an elementary type. The reference type of the access methods' parameters here corresponds to the attribute type that is defined in the persistence representation.

2.4.2 Runtime Behavior

When you instantiate an object that contains a persistent reference, the Persistence Service only loads the explicitly requested object from the database. If the object contains a reference to another persistent object, the Persistence Service checks if it has already loaded this object from the database. If so, the Persistence Service sets a reference to the already loaded object in the instantiated object.

If the Persistence Service hasn't loaded the persistently referenced object yet, it only generates a representative object of the referenced object. This way it recreates the persistent reference, but the referenced object doesn't contain any data yet. The Persistence Service loads the referenced object from the database only when you access the attributes of the referenced object or explicitly instantiate it. So the database is also accessed according to the lazy loading design pattern here, that is, only when you actually need the data.

If the Persistence Service instantiated all persistent references immediately and completely, including all directly referenced objects and at several levels indirectly referenced objects, this could lead to an implicit chain reaction: Instead of only instantiating the single object requested, the Persistence Service might have to instantiate a comprehensive network of objects at once. Particularly if the application requires solely data from an explicitly instantiated object, such behavior will unnecessarily increase the instantiation time, require more memory, and place a higher load on the database system than the approach used in the Persistence Service, that is, loading the referenced objects only when necessary.

2.4.3 Exception Handling

If a persistent object contains a persistent reference to an object that no longer exists, you can read the persistent object that contains the reference from the database and have the access method of the corresponding attribute provide a reference to the representative object of the no longer existing object. In this case, an exception of the CX_OS_OBJECT_NOT_FOUND class only occurs if the Persistence Service attempts to load the no longer existing object from the database. This is usually the case if you access an attribute of the object that no longer exists in the database via an access method.

It's also possible that not only does the referenced object no longer exist but also the entire referenced class. This is also the case if you temporarily delete a persistent class and then recreate an identical class because the system always assigns a new class GUID when creating a class. The Persistence Service can thus no longer determine the class for the obsolete class GUID that may still occur in already-existing persistent references. In this case, the system already raises an exception of the CX_OS_OBJECT_NOT_FOUND class when you instantiate the object that contains the invalid reference. If an invalid class GUID exists in a persistent reference, you can consequently no longer use the Persistent Service to instantiate the object that contains the persistent reference. SAP Note 567253 describes how you can adapt the class GUID of a persistent class in such a constellation.

Another exception situation can occur if you retroactively change the attribute type of a persistent reference. For example, you can use a persistent reference to reference flights and flight bookings if the OBJECT attribute type is set. If you retroactively restrict the attribute type so that only flights can be referenced, already-existing references to flight bookings become invalid. Because in this case the representative object of the referenced object can't be assigned to the attribute with the persistent reference, the system raises an exception already when you instantiate the object that contains the persistent reference.

Here, an exception of the CX_SY_MOVE_CAST_ERROR class is raised in the Persistence Service. However, you can't directly catch this exception outside the Persistence Service because the Persistence Service neither catches nor declares this exception in the parameter interface. Instead, an additional exception of the CX_SY_NO_ HANDLER class is raised. This exception can be caught. Most of the time, this isn't very useful though.

While it frequently can make sense to consider exceptions in an application due to no longer existing objects, automated troubleshooting for invalid class GUIDs or incompatible types of the referenced object is hardly possible. The description of this exception situations given here is supposed to help you avoid the corresponding situations in advance or solve them faster manually when they actually occur.

2.4.4 Limitations for the Use of Persistent References

If the referenced objects don't contain instance GUIDs, you can't use the automated mechanism of persistent references as the Persistence Service provides it. Persistent references are also restricted to mapping n:1 or 1:1 relationships. Object Services don't allow for using persistent references to reference any number of objects from another object based on 1:n or m:n relationships. For example, you can use a persistent reference in a sales order item to reference the superordinate sales order. But references in a sales order to all corresponding items must be managed manually.

2.5   Inheritance

In general, you can map specializations of a class in object-oriented programming via inheritance relationships between classes. When you want to check if a class is supposed to inherit from another class, you should clarify if a so-called *is-a relationship* exists. For example, an electronic flight ticket *is* a flight ticket. Therefore, it can make sense to model an "electronic flight ticket" class as a subclass of a "flight ticket" class. Although a flight ticket shares a lot of information with a flight — the departure and arrival airport, the time of the departure and arrival, for instance — a flight ticket *is no* flight. This means that there's no is-a relationship between the two classes, so a flight ticket and a flight should not have an inheritance relationship in an object-oriented model.

Inheritance relationships between persistent classes basically differ in the effects on the persistence representation of the inheritance between usual ABAP classes. The persistence representation in the context of inheritance relationships can be defined via vertical or horizontal mapping.

2.5.1 Vertical Mapping

In the SAP Help Portal, the persistence representation of several classes that are connected via inheritance relationships is referred to as vertical mapping if parts of the persistence representation are defined both in the superclass and in the subclasses. Here, the persistence representation is implemented using multiple database tables: The superclass defines the mapping of the general attributes that also exist in the objects of all subclasses to a database table with the corresponding fields. Every subclass defines additional individually required attributes as well as the mapping of these attributes to another database table that only contains the corresponding fields for the additionally defined attributes. As already described in Section 2.1.5, Multiple-Table Mapping, all affected database tables must respectively contain fields of the appropriate type for including all components of the key.

Considering the flight ticket example, vertical mapping could look like the example shown in Figure 2.9. The general flight ticket class is mapped to the `STICKET` database table. The special attributes of an electronic ticket, such as an ID number, a credit card number, or a frequent flyer number to identify the customer for the flight, could be mapped to another database table, `/IOT/SETICKET`, which is defined with the same primary key as `STICKET`.

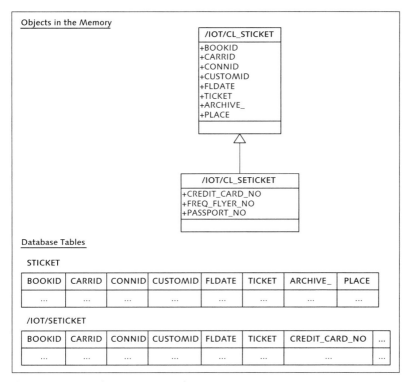

Figure 2.9 Vertical Mapping Example

2.5.2 Horizontal Mapping

If the superclass in an inheritance relationship between persistent classes is an abstract class, you implement a horizontal mapping of the attributes of the classes involved. Like in usual abstract ABAP classes, you can also only define parameter interfaces for individual methods in abstract persistent classes without implementing the methods while you can fully implement other methods. Both in usual and in persistent classes, you can't directly create objects of an abstract class; instead, you have to use concrete subclasses in which all methods are implemented for the creation.

For abstract persistent classes, you can also define the attributes as persistent without having to or being able to specify the mapping of the attributes to the fields of a database table or structure. Instead, you have to implement this mapping in all subclasses that aren't defined as abstract.

Figure 2.10 illustrates the horizontal mapping for an abstract aircraft class with concrete specializations, namely, passenger aircraft and cargo aircraft. In this case, a database table exists that contains the general properties of an aircraft and the specifically defined properties of a passenger aircraft or cargo aircraft, respectively. In case of horizontal mapping, a database table that contains all kinds of aircrafts with their general properties defined in the abstract aircraft class does not exist.

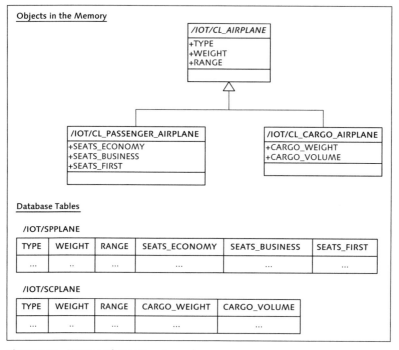

Figure 2.10 Horizontal Mapping Example

The database table for managing the different types of aircrafts in the original SAP flight data model are rather oriented toward vertical mapping. However, you can't map these tables as inheritance relationships using the Persistence Service because the primary keys of the involved database tables are defined by different data elements.

2.5.3   Comparing the Two Mapping Variants

Using horizontal mapping to map the concrete persistent class to a specific database table has the advantage that no resource-intensive access to multiple database tables is necessary to read objects from the database or write objects to the database. In addition, the database indexes enable you to include any combination of fields that are assigned to the general or special class and consequently to further improve the speed of the database accesses.

In case of vertical mapping, a database index can only consist of fields that are assigned to the superclass or of fields that belong to a subclass but not to the superclass. Only vertical mapping enables you to select objects that belong to any subclass in a single database selection.

2.5.4   Type Identifier

If no type identifier is defined in the persistence representation, it isn't immediately clear to which class the object belongs when you instantiate an object via vertical mapping. If you instantiate an object that also belongs to a subclass via the class agent of a superclass without using a type identifier, the class agent returns an object of the superclass. This object then lacks the specialized attributes and the connection to the database table with the specialized fields. With regard to the ticket example, the risk arises that the general ticket part will be deleted so that merely the specialized part of the electronic ticket is kept in the database.

If a field of the `OS_GUID` type with the Type Identifier assignment type is assigned in the persistence representation, the Persistence Service uses this field to store the class GUID of the hierarchically lowest subclass to which the persistent object belongs. Using the type identifier, the instantiation methods of the class agent of the superclass can behave polymorphically (see the next excursus box) and delegate the creation of the object to the responsible class agent of a subclass automatically. E.g., the type identifier would enable the class agent of the ticket superclass to provide a reference to an electronic ticket if you request an electronic ticket using its instantiation methods. You should therefore never implement vertical mapping without a type identifier.

Excursus: Polymorphism

In the context of object-oriented software development, polymorphism refers to the ability of the runtime environment to behave differently at runtime, depending on the type of the object. In conjunction with inheritance hierarchies, this includes the identification of the method that is actually supposed to be executed.

In the example of the general ticket superclass and the specialized subclass of electronic tickets, you can use polymorphism to determine if any ticket type is an electronic ticket. For this purpose, you can define an IS_ETICKET method in the superclass. This method indicates that the ticket isn't an electronic ticket by returning abap_false as the result:

```
METHOD is_eticket.
  re_is_eticket = abap_false.
ENDMETHOD.
```

Only in the subclass of the electronic ticket, you redefine this method so that it returns the abap_true result:

```
METHOD is_eticket.
  re_is_eticket = abap_true.
ENDMETHOD.
```

If you now call the IS_ETICKET method for any ticket object, the system first checks to which class the object belongs at runtime. Only if it's an electronic ticket, the system calls the redefined method, which returns the abap_true result.

2.5.5 Where-Used List for Inheritance Relationships

Irrespective of whether you use Object Services, the where-used list in ABAP in the context of inheritance relationships doesn't always meet the expectations. For example, a where-used list for a method that is inherited from a superclass and hasn't been redefined always provides an empty search result in a subclass. A where-used list for the same method in the superclass in which the method is defined determines all users that call the method even if they explicitly work with a reference to an object of a subclass.

In the ticket example, the where-used list for the GET_FLDATE method that is defined in the /IOT/CL_STICKET superclass doesn't determine any users if executed in the /IOT/CL_SETICKET subclass. A where-used list for the same method in the /IOT/CL_STICKET class determines both the users that call the method with a reference to an object of the /IOT/CL_STICKET class and the users that call the method with a reference to an object of the /IOT/CL_SETICKET class.

For redefined methods, however, a differentiation takes place that can be misleading: The where-used list now differentiates by the type of the users' references. If the list is executed in the superclass, it displays the users that work with a reference of the superclass type; if it's executed in the subclass, it only displays the users that work with a reference of the subclass type. At runtime, however, due to polymorphism only the actual class of the object and not the type of the reference is relevant for the selection of the called method. As a result, the methods of the subclasses are also called from places that the where-used list doesn't display if you execute it for the redefined method in the subclass.

To ensure that you'll definitely find all users of a method, you should execute the where-used list for the method multiple times, once in each class of the inheritance hierarchy.

2.6   Summary

This chapter described some of the functions that the Object Services Persistence Service provides as well as the first steps for the use of the Persistence Service, namely, creating a persistent class, loading objects from the database, and reading attribute values from persistent objects.

This chapter additionally defined the persistence representation. With regard to the persistence representation, you should now have an overview of the entire functional scope of the Persistence Service, including the frequently and less frequently required functions.

The next chapter discusses how you change persistent objects and write these changes to the database.

To implement full-fledged applications, it isn't sufficient to load already existing objects and read their values. Therefore, this chapter describes how you can create new persistent objects and change the values of persistent attributes.

3 Creating and Changing Persistent Objects

This chapter describes how you can create new persistent objects and change already existing persistent objects. The first two sections present methods that initially only affect the objects in the memory of the running program. By means of the Transaction Service, you can write the created and changed persistent objects to the database or undo the implemented changes.

Then you learn about the different management states that a persistent object may have. The management state of a persistent object can change in many actions, for instance, when you instantiate, create, or change the object. In the context of the management states, you also learn how to delete persistent objects, reload already loaded objects from the database, and remove objects from the management of the class agent.

3.1 Creating Persistent Objects

Similar to instantiating a persistent object, there are three methods to create a persistent object (see Section 2.2, Instantiating Persistent Objects, in Chapter 2). Two of these methods are generally defined in the `IF_OS_FACTORY` interface; the Persistence Service defines the third method individually for the respective persistent class. Which methods you can use to create a persistent object depends on the keys that are defined in the persistence representation of the respective persistent class.

None of the methods write the new object to the database immediately. Initially, it is located only in the memory of the running program. Section 3.3, Transaction

Service, details how you can use the Transaction Service to control when the system writes the implemented changes to the database.

After you've created an object, you can no longer change the key of the object. Therefore, when you create objects that use a business key as the primary key, you must specify the primary key that will ultimately be used for the objects. In persistent classes, in which the objects are identified merely via an instance GUID, the Persistence Service automatically assigns the instance GUID during object creation. The instance GUID also cannot be changed after the creation of the object.

3.1.1   IF_OS_FACTORY~CREATE_PERSISTENT

No importing parameters are defined in the parameter interface of the IF_OS_FACTORY~CREATE_PERSISTENT method. The method returns a reference to the newly created persistent object as the return value.

You can only use the method for creating objects of persistent classes in which solely the instance GUID is defined as a key. Because the parameter interface doesn't provide any option to transfer a business key during the call, the Persistence Service doesn't permit the creation of persistent objects with a business key via this method.

Listing 3.1 shows how you can create a persistent object using the IF_OS_FACTORY~CREATE_PERSISTENT method. The reference type of the return value is OBJECT because the method interface is universally defined in the IF_OS_FACTORY interface. When you create a persistent object using this method, you usually need to use the casting operator (?=) to assign the reference to the newly created object to a reference variable with a concrete persistent class as the reference type.

```
DATA: rf_ca_snvoice TYPE REF TO /iot/ca_snvoice,
      rf_snvoice    TYPE REF TO /iot/cl_snvoice.

rf_ca_snvoice = /iot/ca_snvoice=>agent.

rf_snvoice ?=
  rf_ca_snvoice->if_os_factory~create_persistent( ).
```

Listing 3.1 Creating a Persistent Object Using the IF_OS_FACTORY~CREATE_PERSISTENT Method

3.1.2   IF_OS_FACTORY~CREATE_PERSISTENT_BY_KEY

If a business key is defined in the persistence representation of the persistent class, you can create a persistent object using the IF_OS_FACTORY~CREATE_PERSISTENT_ BY_KEY method. You can also call this method of the appropriate class agent for persistent classes whose objects have both a business key and an instance GUID. The only time you cannot use this method is when the instance GUID is defined as the singular key.

The method expects the business key of the persistent object to be created in the form of a structure as the importing parameter. Just like for the IF_OS_CA_ PERSISTENCY~GET_PERSISTENT_BY_KEY method, which you can use to instantiate persistent objects via the business key (see Section 2.2, Instantiating Persistent Objects, in Chapter 2), it is also important for the IF_OS_FACTORY~CREATE_PERSIS- TENT_BY_KEY method that you transfer a structure in which the individual fields of the business key are sorted alphabetically by the field names. Here the Persistence Service also doesn't check whether you actually comply with the sequence. In the worst case, if you transfer an incorrect business key structure, the method creates a persistent object with a business key that is different from the one intended. With such an object, you usually can't continue your work as desired.

Listing 3.2 shows how you can create a persistent object using the IF_OS_ FACTORY~CREATE_PERSISTENT_BY_KEY method. Because the return value is also defined in this method with the OBJECT reference type, a type conversion is carried out using the casting operator (?=).

```
DATA: rf_ca_spfli            TYPE REF TO /iot/ca_spfli,
      rf_spfli               TYPE REF TO /iot/cl_spfli,
      st_business_key_spfli TYPE scol_connection_key.

rf_ca_spfli = /iot/ca_spfli=>agent.

st_business_key_spfli-carrid = 'LH'.
st_business_key_spfli-connid = 4450.

rf_spfli ?=
  rf_ca_spfli->if_os_factory~create_persistent_by_key(
    st_business_key_spfli ).
```

Listing 3.2 Creating a Persistent Object Using the IF_OS_FACTORY~CREATE_PERSISTENT_BY_KEY Method

3.1.3 CREATE_PERSISTENT

Unlike with the two previously discussed methods, you can call the CREATE_ PERSISTENT method in every class agent to create a new object independent of the defined key.

The method receives an importing parameter for each persistent attribute. All values that you transfer to these attributes during the call of the method are directly transferred to the newly created persistent object by the Persistence Service. The importing parameters for value attributes and for persistent references are optional because you can still change the values of these attributes after a persistent object has been created. However, the importing parameters for the components of the business key are mandatory because you cannot change the business key retroactively.

The Persistence Service always automatically assigns the instance GUID when you call the CREATE_PERSISTENT method. Therefore, there is no parameter via which you could specify the value of the instance GUID. In the class agent of a persistent class in which only an instance GUID and no business key is defined, all importing parameters of the CREATE_PERSISTENT method are therefore optional.

In addition to the importing parameters, the parameter interface also contains a return value whose reference type is the respective persistent class. The method returns a reference to the newly created object via the return value.

Listing 3.3 calls the CREATE_PERSISTENT method to create a new flight plan object. The CARRID and CONNID attributes form the business key of the persistent flight plan class, so the calling program of the method must also transfer the two appropriate importing parameters. From the further importing parameters that are defined as optional, Listing 3.3 transfers the departure location and the destination of the flight as an example. The Persistence Service transfers both values to the corresponding attributes already during the creation of the persistent object.

```
DATA: rf_ca_spfli TYPE REF TO /iot/ca_spfli,
      rf_spfli    TYPE REF TO /iot/cl_spfli.

rf_ca_spfli = /iot/ca_spfli=>agent.

rf_spfli =
  rf_ca_spfli->create_persistent(
    i_carrid   = 'LH'
```

```
i_connid   = 4450
i_cityfrom = 'FRANKFURT'
i_cityto   = 'BARCELONA' ).
```

Listing 3.3 Creating a Persistent Object Using the CREATE_PERSISTENT Method

3.1.4   Exception Handling

An exception of the CX_OS_OBJECT_EXISTING class always occurs for the methods for creating a persistent object when you transfer a business key to the respective method and an object with this business key already exists in the management of the class agent. This is the case, for example, if you try to create an object with the same business key several times, or if you've instantiated an object with the same business key before.

Exceptions of the CX_OS_OBJECT_EXISTING class belong to the CX_DYNAMIC_CHECK category. They can occur in the IF_OS_FACTORY~CREATE_PERSISTENT_BY_KEY method and in the CREATE_PERSISTENT method provided that a business key is defined in the persistence representation. Exceptions of this class cannot occur in the IF_OS_FACTORY~CREATE_PERSISTENT method because it always works with a newly created instance GUID.

Because the Persistence Service doesn't write the persistent object to the database during the processing of the method for creating a persistent object, the system doesn't check whether an object exists in the database with an identical business key. So if you use business keys, you must otherwise ensure that you assign each business key to only one persistent object, for example, by using number range objects. If you ensure that the same business key isn't assigned multiple times, it isn't necessary to catch exceptions of the CX_OS_OBJECT_EXISTING class.

An exception of the CX_OS_NO_IMPLEMENTATION class occurs in the IF_OS_ FACTORY~CREATE_PERSISTENT method if a business key is defined in the persistent class. An exception of the same class occurs in the IF_OS_FACTORY~CREATE_PERSIS-TENT_BY_KEY method if no business key is defined in the persistent class.

3.1.5   Creating Transient Objects

For a persistent class, you typically create persistent objects, that is, objects that the Persistence Service stores in the database and that are still available after the running program has terminated. The Persistence Check also provides the option to create transient objects for a persistent class. Whereas you can use transient attributes to define individual attributes that are not saved in the database, you can use a transient object if you do not want to save the object in the database at all. Therefore, transient objects of a persistent class behave similarly to objects of a usual ABAP class: All data that you only store in a transient object is lost when the running program ends.

Similar to creating persistent objects, three methods can be used to create a transient object. Their names include TRANSIENT instead of PERSISTENT. The following methods can be used to create a transient object:

▶ IF_OS_FACTORY~CREATE_TRANSIENT

▶ IF_OS_FACTORY~CREATE_TRANSIENT_BY_KEY

▶ CREATE_TRANSIENT

The Persistence Service doesn't provide a convenient way to convert a transient object into a persistent object retroactively. To achieve this, you would have to read all attributes and temporarily store them in a structure, remove the transient object from the management of the Persistence Service, create a new persistent object, and then transfer all attributes from the structure to the newly created persistent object. If possible, you should prevent this intricate method by creating all objects that you possibly want to write to the database as persistent objects. If you should determine in the course of the program execution that you don't want to write an already-created persistent object to the database, it's easier to use the Transaction Service (see Section 3.3, Transaction Service) or delete the persistent object (see Section 3.4, Management States of Persistent Objects) than to retroactively convert a transient object into a persistent object.

Consequently, the only meaningful area of use for transient objects is the rare case where you don't want to write certain objects of a class to the database, but you do want to store other objects of the same class persistently in the database.

3.2   Changing Attribute Values

For each attribute that you create as a persistent or transient attribute in a persistent class, the Persistence Service automatically generates an access method you can use to read the value of the attribute (see Section 2.3, Instantiating Persistent

Objects, in Chapter 2). For attributes of persistent classes, which are defined as Changeable in the persistence representation, the Persistence Service generates another access method you can use to change the value of the attribute.

The name of the access method for changing an attribute value consists of the SET_ prefix and the name of the attribute. When you call the method, you transfer the new value to which you want to set the attribute.

Listing 3.4 shows the call of a SET method that sets the value of the DISTANCE attribute of a flight plan object to the value that is stored in the v_distance variable.

```
DATA: rf_spfli   TYPE REF TO /iot/cl_spfli,
      v_distance TYPE s_distance.

* Instantiate or create the persistent flight plan object
...

v_distance = 2583.
rf_spfli->set_distance( v_distance ).
```
Listing 3.4 Changing an Attribute Value via a SET Method

The behavior of the SET methods of a persistent class is similar to the behavior of the GET methods: If a persistent object only exists as a representative object in the memory, the Persistence Service tries to read the object from the database when the SET method is called. If the object no longer exists in the database, a SET method triggers an exception of the CX_OS_OBJECT_NOT_FOUND class.

The Persistence Service also marks a persistent object as changed if the transferred value deviates from the previously set attribute value. Provided that this is necessary, the Persistence Service generates a copy of the previous version of the persistent object during the execution of the SET method to be able to recover it later on if required.

Besides the option to change the value of an attribute via the SET method, you can also directly set the value of an attribute in the persistent class itself or in the class agent — also in the subclasses depending on the visibility. In this case, however, the risk exists that you might unknowingly bypass the mechanisms described that apply during the execution of a SET method. This may have the result that the Persistence Service doesn't write the changes to the database, that the Persistence Service overwrites the new values in the running program with old values, or that the functions provided by Object Services to undo changes don't work. To avoid these results, you should implement changes to the values of persistent attributes only via the SET methods.

3.3 Transaction Service

Besides the Persistence Service, the Transaction Service is one of the two original components of Object Services in ABAP. You can use the Transaction Service to control the point in time at which the system writes changes that you've made to the persistent objects to the database. If you determine in a running program that you don't want to write the changes to objects to the database, you can use the Transaction Service to reset the objects to the state they had before the changes.

The Persistence Service and the Transaction Service are closely linked to each other. With the Persistence Service alone — without the Transaction Service — you could load the objects from the database but couldn't write any changes to the objects to the database. Likewise, the Transaction Service alone — without the Persistence Service — provides only few advantages compared to the SAP Logical Units of Work (SAP LUW) known from classical ABAP (see Section 3.3.1, Transactions in SAP Systems). Only the combination of the two services considerably facilitates the development of object-oriented software in ABAP.

3.3.1 Transactions in SAP Systems

The concept *transaction* generally describes multiple sequentially executed steps that form a logical unit collectively. With regard to an information system, this typically includes several changes to data that the system may only execute in combination. If it isn't possible to apply a change that the system should execute within a transaction, the system may not apply any other changes from the transaction.

An example for a transaction is the transportation of material from one storage location to another. Within the transaction that maps this transportation within a system, you must reduce the material stock at the source storage location by the transported quantity and increase the material stock at the target storage location by the same quantity. If you adjust the material stock at one storage location only, this results in an inconsistent state. You can avoid this inconsistent state by using a transaction to ensure that you adjust either both material stocks or no material stocks.

SAP also uses the transaction term for running ABAP programs that were started via a transaction code. During a running program, you can often make completely independent changes to different objects. These changes don't necessarily form a logical unit. Neither do you need to undo all successfully stored changes if a change to an object cannot be executed within a running program. In modern applications, the concept of a transaction in the sense of a logical unit is clearly different from the transaction term used to describe a running program. A running program can consist of a multitude of logical units.

For classic ABAP, SAP uses the concept of *Logical Unit of Work* (LUW) to refer to a logical unit of multiple actions that transfer a system from a consistent state to another state. The database system can form such a LUW if multiple actions are implemented in the database immediately after one another. These *database LUWs* quickly reach their limits when a user must interact with the system between the individual actions in the database.

In classic ABAP, the *SAP LUW* mechanism enables you to combine logically associated actions at the application server level. A new SAP LUW always automatically starts with the start of a program and at the end of the previous SAP LUW in the running program. To end an SAP LUW, you can either use the COMMIT WORK statement to commit all implemented changes permanently or use the ROLLBACK WORK statement to undo all changes implemented in the SAP LUW.

Excursus: SAP Update System

The SAP update system enables you to bundle changing database accesses in the context of SAP LUWs to ensure that the system writes all changes that have accumulated in an SAP LUW to the database directly one after the other in a database LUW. Here, the SAP update system decouples the user dialogs from the process of writing to the database., so the user doesn't have to wait until the system has written all data to the database but can continue to work immediately.

Besides work processes for processing dialog and background applications, every SAP NetWeaver AS ABAP contains at least one identified update process. You can register function modules in your applications that the system executes with COMMIT WORK when you complete an SAP LUW. In this process, the system executes the registered update modules in the sequence in which you registered them in the application.

Using the SAP update system, you can control the number of processes that may write to the database at the same time to either limit the load of the database system or ensure additional parallelism. If multiple update processes are set up, several update processes can simultaneously write changes from an application to the database.

The Transaction Service of Object Services is based on the technology of SAP LUWs from classic ABAP and supplements it with further options. A logical unit, which you create using the Transaction Service, is referred to as a transaction or also an *object-oriented transaction*.

With the update modules and within SAP LUWs, you also have the option to not send changes to the database system until it's determined that you really want to transfer all changes from the SAP LUW. If you use the Persistence Service and the Transaction Service, these services automatically send the changes to the database system at the end of a transaction. Using the Persistence Service and the Transaction Service is considerably easier and more flexible than using update modules.

3.3.2 Object-Oriented Transactions

To combine actions that you carry out in your program in one logical unit using an object-oriented transaction, you must explicitly create a transaction and start this transaction before you make changes to the persistent objects. After you've made changes to the persistent objects, you can decide whether you finish the transaction to permanently accept all changes or whether you want to reset the transaction and undo all changes. Listing 3.5 shows an example for using object-oriented transactions.

```
DATA:
  ri_transaction_manager TYPE REF TO if_os_transaction_manager,
  ri_transaction         TYPE REF TO if_os_transaction.

ri_transaction_manager =
  cl_os_system=>get_transaction_manager( ).

ri_transaction = ri_transaction_manager->create_transaction( ).
ri_transaction->start( ).

* Load, create, change, delete persistent objects
...

ri_transaction->end( ).
```

Listing 3.5 Using Object-Oriented Transactions

Listing 3.5 contains two reference variables: one reference to the Transaction Manager, and one reference to a transaction. You can use the Transaction Manager to create transaction objects and determine already-running transactions. The static method, GET_TRANSACTION_MANAGER, of the CL_OS_SYSTEM class provides a reference to the Transaction Manager. The CL_OS_SYSTEM class contains further static methods by which you can access different central objects of Object Services and make specific settings for the running program.

With the CREATE_TRANSACTION method of the Transaction Manager, you create a new transaction object. The method returns a reference to the new transaction as the return value. This new transaction doesn't affect the running program until you start it using the START method. Therefore, you should always execute the two methods, CREATE_TRANSACTION and START, immediately one after the other.

You should start to load, create, change, or delete persistent objects only after you've created and started a transaction in your application. If you already load persistent objects from the database before you've opened a top-level transaction, Object Services reload these objects from the database after the start of the transaction. Finally, you can permanently commit all implemented changes using the END method of the transaction.

If you call the UNDO method instead of the END method on the transaction object after you've processed persistent objects, the Transaction Service undoes all changes that you've made in the running transaction. The Transaction Service sets all attributes of persistent objects to the value that they had when the START method was called, deletes newly created objects, and restores deleted objects.

The essential difference to the previous mechanism of the SAP LUW is that the UNDO method not only affects the database but also the objects in the memory. The ROLLBACK WORK statement for resetting a SAP LUW, in contrast, only undoes changes to the database. If you work with SAP LUWs without the Transaction Service, you would therefore have to undo all changes to the objects in the memory manually, possibly with additional database accesses. Without the Transaction Service, undoing changes is more tedious both in development and at runtime.

3.3.3 Concatenating Transactions

With each transaction object, you can start and end a transaction exactly once respectively by finishing it with the END method or resetting it with the UNDO method. If you want to implement further actions in a running program after ending a transaction, you therefore require a new transaction object.

To obtain another transaction object, you can either create a new transaction object in the same way as the first transaction object in your application (see Listing 3.6), or you can concatenate the previously running transaction with a new transaction upon termination as in Listing 3.7 by calling the END_AND_CHAIN or the UNDO_AND_ CHAIN concatenate method. The concatenate methods each return a reference to a new already-started transaction.

```
ri_transaction->end( ).
ri_transaction = ri_transaction_manager->create_transaction( ).
ri_transaction->start( ).
```

Listing 3.6 Ending a Running Transaction; Creating and Starting a New Transaction

```
ri_transaction = ri_transaction->end_and_chain( ).
```

Listing 3.7 Ending a Running Transaction and Concatenating It With a New Transaction

The concatenation isn't just an abbreviation to end the old transaction and create and start a new one. The Transaction Service and the Persistence Service also behave differently: Without the concatenation, all persistent objects are only available as representative objects in the memory after you've ended the running transaction and started a new one. The next time a persistent object is accessed, the Persistence Service implicitly reloads the corresponding data from the database. With the concatenation, the persistent objects, including all values of their attributes, remain available after the end of the transaction. In the subsequent transaction, you can continue to work with the persistent objects without the Persistence Service having to read them from the database again.

> **Warning: Calling the Concatenate Methods Correctly**
>
> An error that often occurs when you call the END_AND_CHAIN and UNDO_AND_CHAIN concatenate methods is that the return value of the respective method isn't assigned to the transaction variable. An example of the incorrect call can appear as follows:
>
> ```
> ri_transaction->end_and_chain( ).
> ```
>
> According to this call, ri_transaction references an already-ended transaction that you cannot finish again.
>
> After a correct call, however, the ri_transaction variable references the transaction object that the Transaction Service newly created during the processing of the concatenate method. The example would then look like this:
>
> ```
> ri_transaction = ri_transaction->end_and_chain( ).
> ```

3.3.4 Subtransactions

Besides the previously discussed procedure to not start a new transaction until the previous transaction has been completed, the Transaction Service also provides the option to start another transaction while one transaction already runs. Every transaction that is opened this way is referred to as a subtransaction of the already-running superordinate transaction. However, a top-level transaction is opened if no other transaction is running. Because of this, no superordinate transaction exists for a top-level transaction.

Subtransactions are suitable to subdivide larger logical units of actions into several smaller logical units. For each of these smaller units, the Transaction Service provides the option to undo the changes made to persistent objects.

For example, for a flight booking, you can manage the entire booking as a top-level transaction and combine the individual bookings for outbound flight and return flight in a separate subtransaction. If no seats are available for one flight, you can undo the subtransaction and book an alternative flight in a new subtransaction. After the outbound flight and the return flight have been booked successfully, you can end the top-level transaction and complete the entire flight booking.

The effects of subtransactions are restricted to the persistent objects in the main memory. All changes that you implement without the Persistence Service directly in the database aren't discarded by the system if you reset a subtransaction using the UNDO method. By calling the END method, you initially only confirm the changes that you've implemented in the subtransaction. Here, the Transaction Service changes neither the persistent objects in the memory nor the data in the database.

The sequence shown in Figure 3.1 of a top-level transaction and two subtransactions illustrates the sequence in which you are supposed to start and end the transactions of the flight booking example. The solid line indicates the respective current transaction which you can query from the Transaction Manager via the GET_CURRENT_TRANSACTION method. The current transaction is always the running transaction that you've started last. Running transactions that are superordinate to the current transaction are indicated with a dashed line in Figure 3.1. When you end the current transaction, the superordinate transaction becomes the current transaction again. There is no current transaction prior to the start and after the end of a top-level transaction. You can also use the Transaction Manager to determine the top-level transaction by calling the GET_TOP_TRANSACTION method.

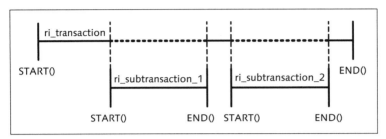

Figure 3.1 Top-Level Transaction and Two Subtransactions

You must end the current transactions in the reverse sequence in which they were started. For an opened subtransaction, you first end the subtransaction and then the superordinate top-level transaction. If you don't follow this sequence and end a top-level transaction while a subtransaction is still running, the method triggers an exception of the CX_OS_TRANSACTION class. As for many exceptions of the CX_DYNAMIC_CHECK category, it makes more sense for you to write the application in such a way that it always ends the transactions in the correct sequence than to implement an exception handling for exceptions of the CX_OS_TRANSACTION class.

3.3.5 Transaction Modes

In your applications, you can use the Transaction Service in two different transaction modes — the object-oriented transaction mode and the compatibility mode. The object-oriented transaction mode is intended for all newly developed, consistently object-oriented applications; the compatibility mode, in turn, is supposed to facilitate the use of Object Services in already-existing applications that work with SAP LUWs directly.

Object-Oriented Transaction Mode

In the object-oriented transaction mode, the application only works with object-oriented transactions. The COMMIT WORK and ROLLBACK WORK statements from classic ABAP are prohibited. The first transaction that you explicitly start in an application becomes the top-level transaction. The examples described before each refer to the object-oriented transaction mode.

Figure 3.2 provides a general overview of how the Transaction Service accesses the classic SAP LUWs within a top-level transaction using the object-oriented transaction mode. While the application creates and starts a transaction, an SAP LUW already runs because the system always automatically starts an SAP LUW when an application is started. If you finish the top-level transaction in an application using the END method, the Transaction Service calls the COMMIT WORK statement when the method is executed. In the same way, the ROLLBACK WORK statement is called when you execute the UNDO method for the top-level transaction.

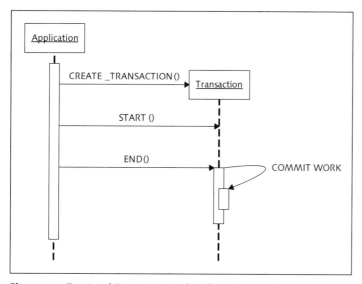

Figure 3.2 Top-Level Transaction in the Object-Oriented Transaction Mode

If you violate the described call hierarchy by calling the COMMIT WORK or ROLLBACK WORK statement directly in your application while you work with transactions in the object-oriented transaction mode, the Transaction Service deliberately triggers a short dump.

Compatibility Mode

In the compatibility mode, the application uses the COMMIT WORK and ROLLBACK WORK statements. The system automatically opens a top-level transaction as soon as you explicitly set the transaction mode or work with a class agent. The application doesn't directly address the top-level transaction. If the application calls the

COMMIT WORK or the ROLLBACK WORK statement, the system notifies — as shown in Figure 3.3 — the Transaction Service that implicitly calls the END or UNDO method of the top-level transaction.

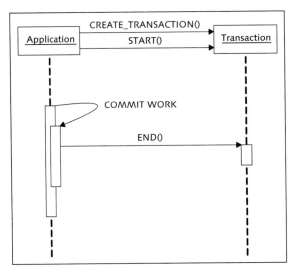

Figure 3.3 Top-Level Transaction in the Compatibility Mode

In the compatibility mode, all transactions with which the application explicitly works are subtransactions of the automatically opened top-level transaction. This way, the system enables you to use the Persistence Service and the Transaction Service also for applications that still work with classic SAP LUWs directly by using the COMMIT WORK and ROLLBACK WORK statements.

Also in the compatibility mode, you must not directly call functions that the system executes implicitly. If you try to finish the top-level transaction directly by calling the END method, the UNDO method, or one of the concatenate methods, the Transaction Service triggers an intended short dump to indicate the error in the application.

Setting the Transaction Mode via the INIT_AND_SET_MODES Method

Before you access Object Services in an internal session for the first time, you must specify the transaction mode in which the application is supposed to run. For this purpose, you can call the static method, INIT_AND_SET_MODES, of the CL_OS_SYS-TEM class and transfer the Boolean parameter, I_EXTERNAL_COMMIT, to it. With this parameter, you specify whether you want to use the COMMIT WORK statement in your application. Therefore, you can transfer abap_false to activate the object-oriented transaction mode (see Listing 3.8) or select the compatibility mode with abap_true (see Listing 3.9).

```
cl_os_system=>init_and_set_modes(
  i_external_commit = abap_false ).
```

Listing 3.8 Activating the Object-Oriented Transaction Mode

```
cl_os_system=>init_and_set_modes(
  i_external_commit = abap_true ).
```

Listing 3.9 Activating the Compatibility Mode

The I_EXTERNAL_COMMIT parameter of the INIT_AND_SET_MODES method is optional. If you call the method without transferring the parameter, the Transaction Service uses the compatibility mode.

Additionally, you must take into account that the system sets the transaction mode implicitly as soon as you access the class agent or the Transaction Manager without having set the transaction mode explicitly. Here as well, the system sets the transaction mode to compatibility mode. Because you may set the transaction mode only once in a running program, the attempt to explicitly set the transaction mode fails afterwards with an exception of the CX_OS_SYSTEM class from the CX_NO_CHECK category. Because of this, you should implement the start of your program in such a ways that it sets the transaction mode as the very first step.

The Transaction Service implicitly sets the compatibility mode so that old applications with SAP LUWs run without any adaptations. However, this should not be considered as a recommendation to use the compatibility mode as often as possible. For new applications, it's recommended to consistently use the object-oriented transaction mode to benefit from the full functional scope of Object Services. You should only refer to the compatibility mode if an existing application already contains complex logic that directly accesses SAP LUWs.

Warning: Frequent Mistake When Setting the Transaction Mode

Before the `INIT_AND_SET_MODES` method is called, the transaction mode must not have been implicitly or explicitly initialized yet. In Listing 3.10, the call fails because this rule is broken twice.

```
DATA: rf_ca_spfli             TYPE REF TO /iot/ca_spfli,
      ri_transaction_manager TYPE REF TO
                                if_os_transaction_manager.

ri_transaction_manager =
  cl_os_system=>get_transaction_manager( ).

cl_os_system=>init_and_set_modes(
  i_external_commit = abap_false ).

rf_ca_spfli = /iot/ca_spfli=>agent.
```

Listing 3.10 Incorrect Call of the INIT_AND_SET_MODES Method After Setting the Transaction Mode

1. The first mistake is that the `GET_TRANSACTION_MANAGER` method is called before the call of the `INIT_AND_SET_MODES` method. The transaction mode is implicitly set within this method. The reverse sequence would lead the calls of the methods to the desired result.

2. The second mistake, which is more difficult to find, is the access to the static attribute, `AGENT`, of a class agent that is made after the call of the `INIT_AND_SET_MODES` method. Before it processes a processing block, for instance, a method, a function module, or an event block in a report, the ABAP runtime environment checks which static attributes and methods the processing block accesses. Before the runtime environment executes the processing block, it calls the class constructors of the classes whose static attributes or methods are accessed by the processing block. In Listing 3.10, the runtime environment initially calls the class constructor of the class agent that implicitly sets the transaction mode. This also has the result that the transaction mode is already set when the `INIT_AND_SET_MODES` method is called.

To solve this problem, you should first call a method when a program is started, whereas this method only sets the transaction mode and then starts a top-level transaction if required. Only then should you call other methods that work with persistent objects or with class agents of persistent classes.

> **Excursus: Class Constructor**
>
> In ABAP, a class constructor is a method that is run through once in each running program before you create an object of the class for the first time or access a static component of the class. Among other things, you can initialize static attributes in the class constructor. For example, within the singleton design pattern you can create an object of the class in the class constructor and store a reference to this object in the static attribute.
>
> There is no consistently used term for the class constructor. In the SAP Help Portal, the class constructor is also referred to as a static constructor. In other programming languages, terms such as class initializer and static initialization block are commonly used for comparable constructs.

Setting the Transaction Mode via the Transaction Code

Besides the option to call a method in the running program, you can also specify the transaction mode when you create a transaction code (Transaction code SE93). If you specify during the creation of a transaction code that you want to use the transaction code to execute a method of a class, you can select the transaction mode in the settings of the transaction code.

In the SAP world, a transaction code that calls a method of a class is also referred to as an *OO transaction*. However, the term isn't to be understood as a synonym for the object-oriented transaction of the Transaction Service nor for the object-oriented transaction mode.

Within the maintenance of the transaction code, SAP uses the term *transaction model* to refer to the transaction mode of the transaction service. If you select the OO Transaction Model checkbox, shown in Figure 3.4, when calling the transaction code, the system automatically sets the object-oriented transaction mode even before the specified method is called. If the checkbox is disabled, the application starts without the initialization of the transaction mode, and you can select the transaction mode yourself in the running program.

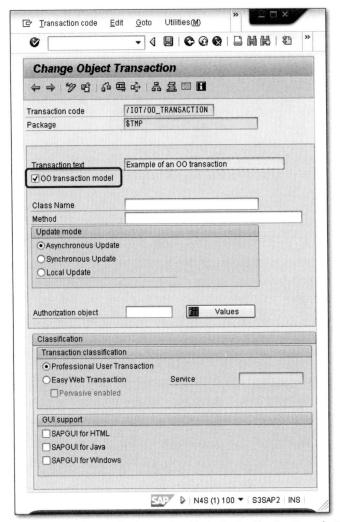

Figure 3.4 Selecting the Transaction Mode During the Creation of a Transaction Code

3.3.6 Update Modes

In addition to the transaction mode, you can also specify an update mode for the Transaction Service. You can use the update mode to control how the system writes the implemented changes to the database after a transaction has been finished. You are provided with four update modes in the object-oriented transaction mode:

- ▸ Direct update
- ▸ Local update
- ▸ Asynchronous update
- ▸ Synchronous update

In case of the direct update and the local update, the Transaction Service writes the data to the database within the same work process in which the application runs. In case of the asynchronous update and the synchronous update, the Transaction Service uses an update process for this purpose. The update modes also differentiate in whether the application already continues running when the transaction ends before the changed data is completely written to the database. Table 3.1 provides an overview of how the update modes differ from the technical point of view. In addition to the name, the list also specifies each update mode's internally used name and the numeric value with which the Transaction Service manages the update mode internally.

Update Mode	SET UPDATE TASK LOCAL	COMMIT WORK AND WAIT	CALL FUNCTION IN UPDATE TASK	Synchronicity
Direct update (DIRECT, 0)	Yes	No	No	Synchronous
Local update (LOCAL, 2)	Yes	No	Yes	Synchronous
Asynchronous update (UPDATE_TASK, 1)	No	No	Yes	Asynchronous
Synchronous update (UPDATE_TASK_SYNC, 3)	No	Yes	Yes	Synchronous

Table 3.1 Overview of the Various Update Modes

The direct update is the only update mode in which the Transaction Service directly calls a method that writes the data to the database. When you set the direct update, the Transaction Service additionally executes the SET UPDATE TASK LOCAL statement. As a result, the system executes all update modules, which you register independently of the Transaction Service, in the same work process in which the statement runs.

When you set the local update, the Transaction Service also executes the SET UPDATE TASK LOCAL statement. Different from the direct update, it doesn't call a method that writes to the database directly. Instead, the Transaction Service registers a function module that the system executes in the same work process as the application when the SAP LUW is finished. Compared to the direct update, this has the result that the system calls all previously registered function modules in the local update and then writes the changes to the persistent objects to the database.

Both for the synchronous and for the asynchronous update, the system executes all registered update modules in a separate work process — an update process. Because the Transaction Service registers an update module in both update modes to write changes to persistent objects to the database, these write database accesses are also implemented in the update process.

The only technical difference between the synchronous and the asynchronous update is that the synchronous update is the only update mode that finishes the SAP LUW not only with the COMMIT WORK statement but also with the AND WAIT addition. Therefore, in the synchronous update, the original work process isn't continued until the update processes have completed all updates. Only in the asynchronous update does the application continue before the Transaction Service has written all changes to the persistent objects to the database.

It's recommended to use the synchronous update if the user is supposed to directly view the result of the update. You should use the asynchronous update if you want to write very large quantities of data to the database because the wait time for the user is omitted, or a background program is already completed while the changes are still written to the database. The local update is more suitable if you only write a small number of objects to the database.

SAP designed the direct update for programs that must not use the CALL FUNCTION IN UPDATE TASK statement. This is usually limited to a few SAP-internal developments. You shouldn't use the direct update for developing applications.

In the compatibility mode, you can select between direct update mode and asynchronous update mode. This enables you to control whether the Persistence Service writes the changes to the database via a simple method call in the running work process or registers an update module for this purpose.

You can also map the behavior of the four update modes of the object-oriented transaction mode in the compatibility mode. For this purpose, select the asynchronous update, call SET UPDATE TASK LOCAL from the application if required, and use COMMIT WORK or COMMIT WORK AND WAIT to decide whether your application is supposed to wait for the execution of the update modules.

Setting the Update Mode

You can set the update mode like the transaction mode via the static method, INIT_AND_SET_MODES, of the CL_OS_SYSTEM class. In this process, you transfer a value to the I_UPDATE_MODE parameter that stands for the update mode in which your application is supposed to run. Suitable constants for the individual update modes are available in the type group, OSCON. Type groups are defined in the data dictionary. They can include data types, constants, and macros. In the OSCON type group, all constants are defined that are used by Object Services. The names of the constants for the update modes start with the OSCON_DMODE_ prefix. You can find the remaining part of the name and the numeric value with which the Transaction Service internally manages the update mode in parentheses under the name of the update mode (Table 3.1). In Listing 3.11, the OSCON_DMODE_UPDATE_TASK_SYNC constant is transferred to the method to select the synchronous update.

```
cl_os_system=>init_and_set_modes(
  i_external_commit = abap_false
  i_update_mode     = oscon_dmode_update_task_sync ).
```

Listing 3.11 Setting the Update Mode

If you don't explicitly decide on an update mode, the application automatically runs with the asynchronous update. Except for the direct update, you can also select the update mode in the definition of a transaction code that calls a method of a class (refer to Figure 3.4).

In contrast to the transaction mode, you can still change the update mode when you start a new top-level transaction in your application. For this purpose, create a new transaction object and transfer the new update mode to the SET_MODE_UPDATE method of the transaction. If you then start this transaction as a new top-level transaction, it runs in the selected update mode.

Exception Handling

The selected update mode also affects the exception behavior when the top-level transaction is completed, provided that Object Services write data to the database.

If you create a new object, and an object with an identical key already exists in the database, Object Services cannot write the newly created object to the database. Also when you change or delete a persistent object, and the same object has already been deleted in the database in the meantime, Object Services cannot transfer the implemented changes to the database successfully. The behavior in these error situations depends on the update mode in which the finished top-level transaction ran.

In the object-oriented transaction mode, an exception occurs in all cases; this exception belongs to the CX_OS_DB superclass and thus to the CX_NO_CHECK category. Only in the direct update could you catch such an exception theoretically. In the local update, there is no option for the application to catch the exception. A short dump occurs in any case. In the synchronous update and the asynchronous update, the exception causes an update error, that is, a short dump in the update process. In the synchronous update, the system informs the running application in the form of an exception of the CX_OS_TRANSACTION class; in the asynchronous update, however, the running application already continues and isn't informed about the update error.

In the compatibility mode, an error in writing the changes always results in a short dump or in an update error when you execute the statement COMMIT WORK or COMMIT WORK AND WAIT. If you use the compatibility mode, none of the update modes provide an option to respond to the error in the running application.

Irrespective of whether a response to an error would theoretically be possible in the update, you should never design your applications in such a way that the changes are written to the database and they may — or may not — work. Chapter 8, Integration of the SAP Lock Concept and Object Services, describes how you can implement applications in systems in which many users simultaneously process the same objects so that you can definitely rule out the previously described error situations.

3.3.7 Check Agents

The Transaction Service provides the mechanism of check agents as an option to carry out any checks for the consistency of changed data. An object that can check its own consistency or the consistency of other objects is referred to as a *check agent*.

To use an object as a check agent, you must implement the IF_OS_CHECK interface in the class to which the object belongs. This may involve a persistent class or a regular class. The interface contains a method called IS_CONSISTENT, whose only parameter is a Boolean return value called RESULT. This method must return abap_true as the return value if the checked object(s) are in a consistent state. In the same way, it must return abap_false if the method detected an inconsistency. Returning abap_false will cause the Transaction Service to not write any changes you made in the running transaction to the database.

Listing 3.12 shows an example for the implementation of a check agent for the flight plan class. In this case, the IF_OS_CHECK interface is implemented directly in the persistent class whose objects are checked. If no departure or destination airport is specified in the persistent object, the method assesses this as an inconsistency and returns abap_false as the result. The method returns the result abap_true only if both airports are specified. At this point, you could carry out many other content-based checks, for instance, whether the specified airports are known in the system or whether the airports are in the countries that are defined as departure or destination countries.

```
METHOD if_os_check~is_consistent.
* Check whether departure and destination airport
* are specified in the flight plan
  IF me->get_airpfrom( ) IS INITIAL OR
     me->get_airpto( ) IS INITIAL.
    result = abap_false.
    RETURN.
  ENDIF.

* Consistency checks have not found any errors
  result = abap_true.
ENDMETHOD.
```

Listing 3.12 Example of a Check Agent Implementation

The Transaction Service automatically calls the checks of a check agent when a transaction is finished if you previously registered the check agent in the running transaction. For this purpose, call the REGISTER_CHECK_AGENT method, and transfer an object to the method that belongs to a class that implements the check agent interface. Within the execution of the END and END_AND_CHAIN methods, the Transaction Service calls all check agents that are registered in the transaction. As soon as the first check agent notifies an inconsistency in the form of the return value abap_false, the Transaction Service will stop calling the other registered check agents.

Instead, the Transaction Service informs the caller of the END method in the form of an exception of the CX_OS_CHECK_AGENT_FAILED class that an inconsistency exists. Then, it's theoretically possible to correct the inconsistency and call the END method again on the same transaction. In the repeated call, the system would pass through all check agents again. Usually, it makes more sense to cancel the changes summarized in the transaction by calling the UNDO method if an inconsistency occurs.

Listing 3.13 contains all components that you normally require in your application for using check agents. During the running transaction, the application registers a newly created flight plan object as a check agent. If the check agent notifies an inconsistency, the application responds by cancelling the transaction instead of finishing it.

```
DATA:
  ri_transaction_manager TYPE REF TO if_os_transaction_manager,
  ri_transaction         TYPE REF TO if_os_transaction,
  rf_ca_spfli            TYPE REF TO /iot/ca_spfli,
  rf_spfli               TYPE REF TO /iot/cl_spfli.

* Create and start transaction
ri_transaction_manager =
  cl_os_system=>get_transaction_manager( ).

ri_transaction = ri_transaction_manager->create_transaction( ).
ri_transaction->start( ).

* Create new flight plan object
rf_ca_spfli = /iot/ca_spfli=>agent.

rf_spfli =
  rf_ca_spfli->create_persistent(
    i_carrid = 'LH'
    i_connid = 4450 ).

* Register flight plan as a check agent for the
* running transaction
ri_transaction->register_check_agent( rf_spfli ).
```

```
* Specify departure and destination airport
rf_spfli->set_airpfrom( 'FRA' ).
rf_spfli->set_airpto( 'BCN' ).

* Finish transaction
TRY.
    ri_transaction->end( ).
  CATCH cx_os_check_agent_failed.
*    Reset transaction because check agent
*    has found inconsistencies
    ri_transaction->undo( ).
ENDTRY.
```

Listing 3.13 Using a Check Agent from the Perspective of an Application

3.3.8 Undo Mechanism for Persistent Objects

The undo mechanism is the function of the Transaction Service used to return changed persistent objects to the original state when a transaction is reset. The undo mechanism is activated by default for most transactions.

The Transaction Service automatically deactivates the undo mechanism only for the implicitly opened top-level transaction in the compatibility mode. Even if the undo mechanism was activated in the compatibility mode, you couldn't benefit from it. Because you have no option in the compatibility mode to finish the top-level transaction with a concatenate method, the database reloads all objects with the next access after finishing a top-level transaction.

If you can already foresee that you don't require the undo mechanism for certain transactions, you can disable it explicitly. For this purpose, call the SET_MODE_UNDO_RELEVANT method after the creation but before the start of a transaction, and transfer the abap_false value as the parameter to the method. If you then use one of the concatenate methods, the Transaction Service uses this setting for the subsequent transaction.

If the undo mechanism is disabled, a top-level transaction behaves similarly to a classic SAP LUW; that is, you can undo changes in the database by resetting the transaction, but you cannot return objects in the memory to a previous state. Sub-transactions — apart from the option of registering check agents — are completely meaningless if you disable the undo mechanism because neither the END nor the UNDO method have any effect on objects in the memory or on data in the database if the undo mechanism is switched off.

> **Warning: Disabling the Undo Mechanism for a Subtransaction**
>
> If you disable the undo mechanism for a transaction, Object Services may write changes to the database that you tried to discard.
>
> Changes to a persistent object that you implement within a transaction with the undo mechanism disabled remain even if you execute the UNDO method on a subtransaction or execute the UNDO_AND_CHAIN method on any transaction. If you then finish the top-level transaction with the END method or the SAP LUW with the COMMIT WORK statement, Object Services also write those changes to the database that you made in the reset subtransaction.

Only for the top-level transaction in the object-oriented transaction mode can it sometimes be helpful to disable the undo mechanism. The undo mechanism for the top-level transaction is already disabled in the compatibility mode. If you consider disabling the undo mechanism for a subtransaction, you should ask yourself what you actually require the subtransaction for.

Your application runs a little bit faster if the undo mechanism is disabled and requires less memory. However, the benefits are low so that you shouldn't change your applications to be able to work without the undo mechanism. Only disable the undo mechanism if your application can't benefit from it.

3.3.9 Transaction Statuses

Every transaction object with which you work in your application contains a status attribute that describes the state of the transaction in more detail. For example, the Transaction Service uses the transaction status to prevent the same transaction from being finished multiple times.

In your application, you can read the current status of a transaction via the instance method, GET_STATUS. You can also have the system display the TRANSACTION_STATE attribute in the debugger to track the current transaction status in the running program.

The Transaction Service manages the transaction status in the form of an integer variable with possible values between 0 and 5. The OSCON type group contains a constant with a readable name for every possible transaction status. The names of the constants for the transaction statuses start with the OSCON_TSTATUS_ prefix.

Figure 3.5 shows the transaction states and the possible transitions between the states. The parentheses behind the name of the status indicate the integer value that the Transaction Service uses to manage the state internally. Figure 3.5 intentionally excludes the END_REQ status that is internally managed with the value 2 because it only occurs temporarily during the processing of the END method and is normally not visible for applications.

After you've created a transaction via the CREATE_TRANSACTION method in the Transaction Manager, every transaction is initially in the NEW status. Immediately after the creation, you should start the transaction via the START instance method and thus bring it to the RUNNING state. After you've executed all actions that you want to combine in the transaction, either finish the transaction via the END method, or undo the changes via the UNDO method.

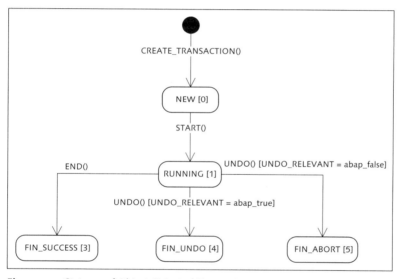

Figure 3.5 Statuses of Object-Oriented Transactions

After a successful execution of the END method, the transaction is in the FIN_SUCCESS status. However, if an exception occurs in the execution of the END method, for example, because a check agent notifies an inconsistency, the transaction remains in the RUNNING status. When you execute the UNDO method, the Transaction Service takes into account whether the undo mechanism is activated. If the Transaction Service can restore the old state, the transaction ends in the FIN_UNDO status or otherwise in the FIN_ABORT status. A return to the previous states isn't intended from the three final states. You need to use a new transaction object to summarize further actions.

The concatenate methods, END_AND_CHAIN and UNDO_AND_CHAIN, have the same effect on the transaction on which they are executed as the methods END or UNDO. Additionally, they return a new transaction object as the return parameter. This object is already in the RUNNING status.

3.4 Management States of Persistent Objects

The Persistence Service manages a management state for every persistent object that is located in the memory of the running application. By means of this management state, it can determine which objects have changed and how, and how it has to write these changes to the database. For example, the Persistence Service must create a new data record in the database for a newly created persistent object; for a changed persistent object, however, it adjusts an existing data record.

Methods of the persistent class, methods of the associated class agent and the object-oriented transactions affect the management state of a persistent object. Even if you don't work with transactions directly in the compatibility mode, the implicitly managed top-level transaction affects the management state of persistent objects in the memory if you finish an SAP LUW.

To determine the current management state of a persistent object, you can call the IF_OS_CA_INSTANCE~GET_STATUS method of the associated class agent. To this method of the class agent, you transfer a reference to the persistent object whose management state you want to determine. As a result, you get a numeric value between 0 and 12 that stands for a management state. For every management state, you can find a constant in the OSCON type group; the name of this constant starts with the prefix OSCON_OSTATUS_.

Whether a persistent object already resides in the database has major influence on the possible transitions between the individual management states, so the following sections initially describe the possible transitions for objects that don't exist in the database yet. This is followed by the description of possible transitions for objects that already exist in the database. Then you learn about the transitions when transactions and SAP LUWs are completed. Only at these points, Object Services create persistent objects in the database and delete them from the database. The state transitions at these points therefore form the link between the transitions for persistent objects that don't exist in the database yet and the transitions for persistent objects that already exist in the database.

3.4.1 State Transitions for Persistent Objects That Don't Exist in the Database Yet

Figure 3.6 shows the possible transitions for persistent objects that don't exist in the database yet, that is, for objects that you've created in the running program using one of the CREATE_PERSISTENT methods or one of the CREATE_TRANSIENT methods.

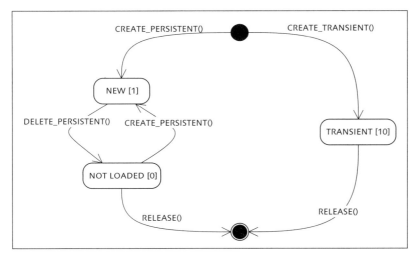

Figure 3.6 State Transitions for Persistent Objects That Don't Exist in the Database Yet

After the creation, a persistent object is in the NEW management state as long as it doesn't exist in the database yet. During a running transaction, the object only leaves this management state if you delete it explicitly. For this purpose, you call the class agent's DELETE_PERSISTENT method that is defined in the IF_OS_FACTORY interface and transfer a reference to the persistent object to this method. Alternatively, you can also use the DELETE_PERSISTENT method that is directly defined in the class agent. To this method, you transfer the key of the object to be deleted instead of a reference to the persistent object. After deletion, the persistent object is in the NOT LOADED state. In this state, the persistent object only exists as a representative object in the memory of the running application; that is, the attributes of the object aren't filled.

After deletion, you can create a persistent object with the same key again or remove it completely from the management of the class agent in the running application.

Just like IF_OS_FACTORY~DELETE_PERSISTENT, the RELEASE method is defined in the IF_OS_FACTORY interface and implemented in every class agent. To it, you can pass a reference to an object, which, compared to the original state in the database, you haven't changed. After the call of the RELEASE method, the class agent behaves as if you've never instantiated or created the object. This is represented by the final state shown previously in Figure 3.6.

The possible transitions for transient objects are much easier to comprehend. After creation, a transient object is in the TRANSIENT state. Because a transient object never exists permanently, you cannot delete it explicitly. Instead, you can directly remove it from the management of the class agent via the RELEASE method.

3.4.2 State Transitions for Persistent Objects That Already Exist in the Database

Figure 3.7 shows the possible state transitions for persistent objects that already exist in the database. In addition to the NOT LOADED state for persistent objects that already exist in the database, possible management states are LOADED for loaded objects, CHANGED for changed objects, and DELETED for deleted objects.

The Persistence Service transfers objects, which you instantiate via one of the GET_PERSISTENT methods, to the LOADED state. If an instantiated object contains persistent references to other persistent objects that aren't instantiated yet, the Persistence Service creates the referenced objects as representative objects, that is, in the NOT LOADED state.

The REFRESH_PERSISTENT method from the IF_OS_FACTORY interface provides another option to transfer a persistent object to the NOT LOADED state. If you transfer an already loaded, persistent object to this method of the corresponding class agent, the class agent discards the values of all attributes of the object and marks it as a representative object. As a result, the Persistence Service loads the object from the database again with the next access to an attribute of the object or if you call a GET_PERSISTENT method again. This way, the REFRESH_PERSISTENT method indirectly allows you to reload a persistent object from the database if required.

If you change a value of an attribute of a persistent class via a SET method, the object is then in the CHANGED state. If the object was previously available as a representative object in the memory, the Persistence Service initially loads the object from the database within the SET method. A transition from NOT LOADED to LOADED is also possible with a SET method, namely, if the object was previously available as a representative object in the memory and the alleged changed attribute was already set to the transferred value.

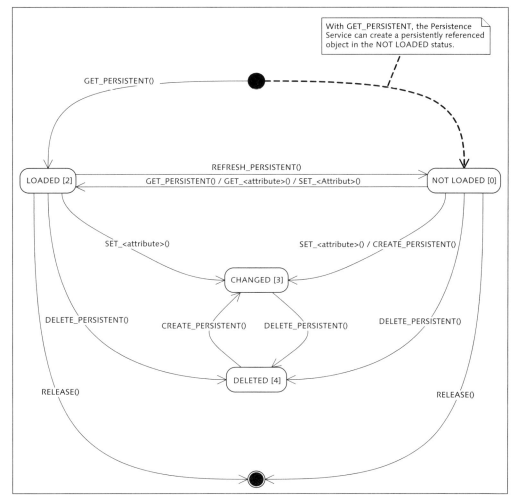

Figure 3.7 State Transitions for Persistent Objects That Already Exist in the Database

Apart from already deleted objects, you can delete persistent objects in any state. The IF_OS_FACTORY~DELETE_PERSISTENT and DELETE_PERSISTENT methods, respectively, mark the persistent object as deleted in the memory. The associate data record still exists in the database until you end the top-level transaction or the SAP LUW.

With the RELEASE method, you also remove an object that already exists in the database from the management of the class agent of the running program. In this process, you don't delete the object from the database. Therefore, you can instantiate it again at a later stage.

After you've marked an object as deleted, you can use a CREATE_PERSISTENT method to create a new persistent object with the same key. The Persistence Service interprets such a process as a change of an existing object. In the memory of your application, the Persistence Service doesn't create a new object but adjusts the existing one. In this case, the persistent object is therefore in the CHANGED state after the execution of a CREATE_PERSISTENT method, and all possibly still existing references to the deleted object in your application refer to the newly created object.

You can obtain a semantically surprising result if you call a CREATE_PERSISTENT method with the key of an object that is available in the database and exists as a representative object in the memory. Actually, you don't create a persistent object but overwrite the already-existing object with data that you transfer to the CREATE_PERSISTENT method. To not trigger this mechanism accidentally, it's recommended to always call a GET_PERSISTENT method after the execution of the REFRESH_PERSISTENT method if you want to load the data for an object from the database again.

Changes to Values of Transient Attributes

With the default settings of the Persistence Service, the transition from the LOADED state to the CHANGED state not only occurs if you change a persistent attribute with a SET method, but also when you change a transient attribute. Because the CHANGED state causes Object Services to write the persistent object to the database when the top-level transaction is being completed, it can happen that you write persistent objects to the database again even though you've only changed transient attributes.

Because transient attributes aren't written to the database by definition, you therefore rewrite an unchanged object to the database. Particularly if you instantiate many persistent objects and in doing so initialize their transient attributes via SET methods with meaningful values, and then finish the transaction without having changed persistent attributes of the objects, this unnecessarily results in a considerable higher load of the database.

With the support package stacks that have been published since 2006 (Support Package Stack 16 for Release 6.40, Support Package Stack 6 for Release 7.0), SAP provides an enhancement of the Persistence Service with which you can disable this behavior. In the generator settings for the persistence representation, you can now select the "Changes to Transient Attributes Do Not Cause Saving of Persistent Attributes" option (see Figure 3.8). You can find the generator settings in the persistence representation dialog via the GOTO • GENERATOR SETTING menu path or using the F5 key.

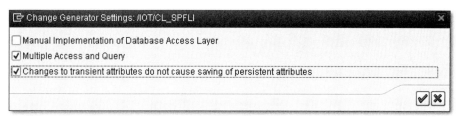

Figure 3.8 Generator Settings of the Persistence Service

If you've activated this generator setting, the persistent objects remain in the LOADED condition when you change the value of a transient attribute via a SET method. Even though this setting doesn't provide major advantages in each case, it doesn't result in any disadvantages either, so you should activate the setting in every persistent class. The setting is already activated by default in persistent classes that you create on SAP NetWeaver AS ABAP as of Release 7.0 EhP2.

If you work with an older release in which the setting isn't available yet, as a workaround you can write your own method which you can use to change the value of the transient attribute. Here, you can build the parameter interface as in a SET method. However, you need to select a name that doesn't start with SET. Before you set the transient attribute to the transferred value in such a method, you should call the STATE_WRITE_ACCESS macro. Among other things, the macro loads the persistent object from the database if it's a representative object. Listing 3.14 provides an implementation example of such a method for a transient attribute with the name CARRIER_NAME.

```
METHOD write_carrier_name.
* Inform class agent about upcoming write access
  state_write_access.

* Change value of transient attribute
  me->carrier_name = im_carrier_name.
ENDMETHOD.
```
Listing 3.14 Method for Changing a Transient Attribute

3.4.3 State Transitions When Finishing Transactions and SAP Logical Units of Work

Every object-oriented transaction can affect the management state of a transient object at two points in time: at its start and at its end.

▸ At the start of a new top-level transaction, Object Services roll back all persistent objects to the NOT LOADED state. If you've changed, created, or deleted an object while no top-level transaction was opened, these changes are lost when a top-level transaction is started. Transient objects, however, remain in the TRANSIENT state because the Persistence Service cannot reload them from the database if required. The start of a subtransaction has no effects on the management state of persistent or transient objects either.

▸ If you end a top-level transaction with the END method, Object Services write all changes to the database that you made in the transaction. Here, the management state of the persistent objects remains unchanged until you start a new transaction. Also when you end a subtransaction with the END method, the management states of all persistent objects remain the same.

The effects of the UNDO method depend on whether the undo mechanism is activated for the reset transaction. If the undo mechanism is activated, both for top-level transactions and for subtransactions, Object Services restore the state that the persistent objects had at the beginning of the transaction. This applies to the values of the objects' attributes and to the management state. To not have to load the same objects from the database too often, the objects that you've loaded from the database during the running transaction remain in the LOADED state even if they were in the NOT LOADED state before the start of the transaction. Even if you load persistent objects and then change the attributes or delete the persistent object, the UNDO method transfers these objects to the

LOADED state. If you have deactivated the undo mechanism, however, all persistent objects remain in the same management state both in the UNDO method and in the END method.

The statements for ending classic SAP LUWs — COMMIT WORK and ROLLBACK WORK — have the same effect on management statements of persistent objects as if you finished a top-level transaction with the END method or the UNDO method and then started a new top-level transaction: Object Services transfer all persistent objects to the NOT LOADED state. Because the undo mechanism is switched off for the top-level transaction in the compatibility mode, a transient object remains in the TRANSIENT state even if you create it in an SAP LUW and reset the SAP LUW with the ROLLBACK WORK statement.

By contrast, the concatenate methods, END_AND_CHAIN and UNDO_AND_CHAIN, behave differently if you execute them on a top-level transaction. Here, the basic principle is that all persistent objects that are loaded and continue to exist remain loaded while all other objects become a representative object. For both concatenate methods, the objects with the LOADED and CHANGED states end in the LOADED state because both loaded and changed objects continue to exist after finishing a transaction either using the END_AND_CHAIN or the UNDO_AND_CHAIN method.

However, the behavior for objects differs in the NEW and DELETED states. The END_AND_CHAIN method creates objects in the database that are in the NEW state and deletes objects that are in the DELETED state. Consequently, objects pass from the NEW state to the LOADED state or from DELETED to NOT LOADED. The UNDO_AND_CHAIN method undoes both the creation and the deletion of objects. So, persistent objects change from the NEW state to the NOT LOADED state. For objects from the DELETED states, the target state depends on whether the persistent object was loaded from the database. If the object was loaded, it can transfer to the LOADED state; otherwise, the NOT LOADED state arises here.

Due to the varying behavior, in the object-oriented transaction mode, you should decide for your applications whether it makes more sense to end the top-level transaction and start a new one, or whether you should use a concatenate method. If you end the running top-level transaction and then start a new transaction, the Persistence Service will load the current state from the database for all loaded persistent objects after the top-level transaction has been ended. This way, you don't need to call the REFRESH_PERSISTENT method for every persistent object that you want to load from the database when you start a new transaction. If you want to continue with the previously loaded state in the subsequent transaction, use the concatenate methods. It reduces the load of the database system and ensures that the applications run faster.

If you need to use the compatibility mode, you don't have a corresponding choice. Object Services reload the persistent objects in every new SAP LUW from the database as soon as you access them.

3.5   Summary

After learning about the Persistence Service in Chapter 2, this chapter introduced you to the second service of Object Services: the Transaction Service. You can use the Persistence Service and the Transaction Service to make changes to persistent objects, and you learned how these changes affect the management state of persistent objects.

The next chapter discusses the Query Service, thus completing the description of all functions that are currently provided by Object Services.

Various options are available for identifying persistent objects that meet certain criteria. This chapter introduces these options, including classic Open SQL and the Object Services Query Service.

4 Selecting Persistent Objects

The previous chapters described how you can instantiate objects whose keys — that is, either their business keys or their instance GUIDs — you already know. In real life, however, you often have to instantiate objects whose keys you don't know. This chapter explains how to instantiate all objects that meet certain criteria. Criteria can be, for example, a part of a composed key, specific values or value ranges of attributes, or the class to which the objects belong.

4.1 Determining Keys of Persistent Objects with Open SQL

Open SQL statements, which are integrated in ABAP and can be used independently of the database system, enable you to determine the keys of the objects that you want to instantiate. You can thus instantiate all objects that meet specific criteria without having to use other components of Object Services than the ones already introduced.

Listing 4.1 follows this approach. A `SELECT` query in Open SQL first determines the business keys of all flights from the SAP flight data model that take place at the current date and temporarily stores them in an internal table. In a `LOOP` loop for the internal table of the business keys, the class agent then instantiates the corresponding persistent object in each loop run for a business key using the `IF_OS_CA_PERSISTENCY~GET_PERSISTENT_BY_KEY` method. An additional internal table finally stores the references to the instantiated persistent objects.

```
DATA:
  rf_ca_sflight              TYPE REF TO /iot/ca_sflight,
  rf_flight                  TYPE REF TO /iot/cl_sflight,
```

```
    ta_business_keys_flights TYPE STANDARD TABLE OF
                                     scol_flight_key,
    ta_rf_flights            TYPE STANDARD TABLE OF
                                     REF TO /iot/cl_sflight,
    wa_business_key_flight   TYPE scol_flights_key.

rf_ca_sflight = /iot/ca_sflight=>agent.


* Determine business keys of all flights with today's date
* with an Open SQL query
SELECT carrid connid fldate
        INTO CORRESPONDING FIELDS OF TABLE
              ta_business_keys_flights
        FROM sflight
        WHERE fldate = sy-datum.


* Instantiate for each business key the corresponding
* persistent object separately
LOOP AT ta_business_keys_flights INTO wa_business_key_flight.
  rf_flight ?=
    rf_ca_sflight->if_os_ca_persistency~get_persistent_by_key(
      wa_business_key_flight ).
  APPEND rf_flight TO ta_rf_flights.
ENDLOOP.
```

Listing 4.1 Instantiating All Flights on the Current Date with Open SQL and the GET_
PERSISTENT_BY_KEY Method

Before Release 7.0 of SAP NetWeaver AS ABAP, the combination of an Open SQL statement and an instantiation that is implemented for each object separately was the only option to instantiate all persistent objects that meet specific criteria. As of Release 7.0, SAP NetWeaver AS ABAP delivers two new alternatives for instantiating multiple persistent objects.

Since then, the class agents of persistent classes have provided two new mass instantiation methods. These methods enable you to use one method call to instantiate the persistent objects for multiple already known keys.

Even more comprehensive are the innovations that a third newly introduced method in the class agent provides. You pass an object that contains conditions to this method. This object is called a *query*. The method then instantiates all persistent objects that meet the conditions of the query. You don't have to use Open

SQL statements in your application in this case. The functions for formulating and executing queries are referred to as the Query Service. The Persistence Service, the Transaction Service, and the Query Service constitute the three current Object Services components.

4.2   Mass Instantiation

To instantiate persistent objects for multiple already known keys, every class agent contains a method to which you can pass an internal table with business keys or instance GUIDs. Like Listing 4.1, Listing 4.2 instantiates all flights on the current date. The business keys of the persistent objects again are determined by an Open SQL statement. Then, the `GET_PERSISTENT_BY_KEY_TAB` method from the `IF_OS_CA_PERSISTENCY` interface is called. This method tries to load the appropriate persistent object from the database for every transferred business key. The method returns an internal table with references to the instantiated persistent objects. The reference to a persistent object is respectively specified in the result table in the same line that contained the appropriate key in the transferred table.

```
DATA: rf_ca_sflight            TYPE REF TO /iot/ca_sflight,
      ta_business_keys_flights TYPE STANDARD TABLE OF
                                    scol_flights_key,
      ta_ro_flights            TYPE osreftab.

rf_ca_sflight = /iot/ca_sflight=>agent.

* Determine business keys of all flights with today's date
* with an Open SQL query
SELECT carrid connid fldate
       INTO CORRESPONDING FIELDS OF TABLE
            ta_business_keys_flights
       FROM sflight
       WHERE fldate = sy-datum.

* Instantiate for each business key the corresponding
* persistent object
ta_ro_flights =
  rf_ca_sflight->if_os_ca_persistency~get_persistent_by_key_tab(
    ta_business_keys_flights ).
```

Listing 4.2 Instantiating All Flights on the Current Date with Open SQL and the GET_PERSISTENT_BY_KEY_TAB Method

The GET_PERSISTENT_BY_KEY_TAB method is available in the class agents of all persistent classes for which you have defined a business key in the persistence representation. The transferred internal table can be a standard table or a sorted table. The line type of the table must correspond to the business key structure of the persistent class. In this context, remember that you have to use a structure in which the individual components are sorted by attribute names (see the warning box in Section 2.2.2, IF_OS_CA_PERSISTENCY~GET_PERSISTENT_BY_KEY, of Chapter 2).

The return value of the method is of the OSREFTAB type. This is a standard table in which each line contains a reference of the OBJECT type. In case of later accesses to the persistent objects, downcasting is required here.

Similar to the GET_PERSISTENT_BY_KEY_TAB method, the class agent contains the GET_PERSISTENT_BY_OID_TAB method, which enables you to instantiate multiple persistent objects via their respective instance GUID. You can use the method in the class agent of persistent classes in whose persistence representation an instance GUID is defined. You pass a standard table or a sorted table with the OS_GUID line type to the method and also receive a result of the OSREFTAB type by this method.

The extent to which you can improve the speed, which can be achieved by implementing mass instantiation instead of calling the instantiation of one persistent object respectively several times (see Listing 4.1), depends on the system and the type of the objects used. Considerable speed improvements of more than 50% as well as a runtime behavior that hardly differs in both variants have been observed. As of Support Package 13 for SAP NetWeaver AS ABAP 7.0, however, the process speed of the mass instantiation has in general always been as high as the speed of the separately called instantiation process. In previous releases (due to an error that has been eliminated in the meantime), it was possible that the mass instantiation process, if more than 500 persistent objects were instantiated in parallel, ran slower than the instantiation process that is subsequently called for individual objects several times.

The methods for the mass instantiation only raise an exception of the CX_OS_OBJECT_NOT_FOUND class if they detect an object that is in the DELETED or TRANSIENT management state for a transferred key. In an attribute, the exception object contains the business key or instance GUID of the object for which the exception was raised. If such an exception occurs, the corresponding method terminates the instantiation of further persistent objects for the transferred keys.

If you pass a key for which no object exists in the database to a method for mass instantiation, this doesn't raise an exception as it's the case for an instantiation of individual objects. The instantiation of further objects is also not terminated in this case. Instead, the result table contains a null reference in the corresponding line. For example, if you pass a key to the method in the third line of the table, and the method can't find a persistent object for this key in the class agent management or in the database, the result table contains a null reference and not a reference to a persistent object in the third line. Each line of the result table for which you have passed a key of an existing persistent object contains a valid reference.

4.3   Simple Selections Using the Query Service

Besides mass instantiation that enables you to instantiate multiple persistent objects for already known keys, Object Services also provide the option for instantiating all persistent objects whose persistent attributes meet certain conditions. The Query Service helps you formulate a query in which you define a filter condition specifying the conditions that the persistent attributes of the persistent objects are supposed to meet. You can also define a sort condition of a query according to which criteria the system is supposed to sort the persistent objects.

There are two options for formulating the filter condition and the sort condition: You can use a syntax that is similar to the WHERE or ORDER BY clauses of an SQL query, and you can define filter and sort conditions using objects. This alternative way of formulating conditions is described in Section 4.4, More Complex Selections Using the Query Service.

Listing 4.3 provides an example of how you can implement the determination of all flights on the current date. Here, the flights are determined and instantiated using the Query Service.

```
DATA: rf_ca_sflight     TYPE REF TO /iot/ca_sflight,
      ri_query_manager  TYPE REF TO if_os_query_manager,
      ri_query          TYPE REF TO if_os_query,
      ta_ro_flights     TYPE osreftab,
      v_filter          TYPE string.
```

```
rf_ca_sflight = /iot/ca_sflight=>agent.
ri_query_manager = cl_os_system=>get_query_manager( ).

* Formulate filter condition and create query
CONCATENATE 'FLDATE = ''' sy-datum '''' INTO v_filter.
ri_query =
  ri_query_manager->create_query(
    i_filter = v_filter ).

* Instantiate all persistent objects that correspond to the
* conditions of the query
ta_ro_flights =
  rf_ca_sflight->if_os_ca_persistency~get_persistent_by_query(
    ri_query ).
```

Listing 4.3 Instantiating All Flights on the Current Date Using the Query Service

Creating a query of the Query Service is similar to creating a transaction of the Transaction Service: The static method of the CL_OS_SYSTEM class (here: GET_QUERY_ MANAGER) provides you with a reference to the Query Manager. The Query Manager provides a method called CREATE_QUERY, which creates a new query and returns a reference to this query. You can pass the filter conditions and sort conditions to the CREATE_QUERY method when creating the query, or you can set them via various methods of the query object after you have created the query (see Section 4.4, More Complex Selections Using the Query Service).

When formulating the filter and sort conditions, you have to refer to the names of the persistent attributes respectively. If you've assigned the same names to the persistent attribute in the persistence representation as to the field in the database table, this isn't a potential source of error. However, if you've defined attributes names in the persistence representation that aren't identical to the field names in the database table, you have to take extra care to use the attribute names instead of the field names of the underlying database table when formulating the filter and sort criteria. Also, in filter and sort conditions, you're only allowed to use persistent attributes for which you have selected the Public visibility in the persistence representation.

After defining the desired filter and sort conditions for the query, call the IF_OS_ CA_PERSISTENCY~GET_PERSISTENT_BY_QUERY method of the class agent of the class for which you want to instantiate the persistent objects. To this method, you must pass the query object in which you defined the filter and sort conditions.

You can modify the behavior of the IF_OS_CA_PERSISTENCY~GET_PERSISTENT_BY_ QUERY method using the I_UPTO and I_SUBCLASSES parameters:

▶ The I_UPTO parameter enables you to specify how many persistent objects the method is supposed to return as a maximum. This way, you can limit the number of instantiated objects and consequently the application's load time and memory consumption. This is particularly useful if you allow the user to define the filter condition, and numerous persistent objects are available for the persistent class.

If the number of persistent objects that meet the filter condition is greater than the value of I_UPTO, the method provides a subset of the persistent objects that meet the filter condition. If you've specified a sort condition, the method provides the first persistent objects sorted according to this condition. If you haven't defined a sort condition, you shouldn't make any assumptions of how the Query Service selects the returned subset of objects. If you don't use the I_UPTO parameter or pass the 0 value, the number of returned objects won't be limited. You shouldn't pass negative values to the parameter.

▶ The I_SUBCLASSES parameter is only relevant if subclasses exist for the persistent class and if you've defined a type identifier in the persistence representation. If you pass the abap_true value to this parameter, the method also instantiates the objects of the persistent class, which simultaneously belong to a subclass of the persistent class. If a type identifier does exist, the method has a polymorphic behavior; that is, it will return objects of the subclasses automatically. Attributes that are defined in subclasses are also filled in this case, even if you've called the method in the class agent of the superclass. If the default setting, abap_false, is used and a type identifier is specified, the method only returns persistent objects that belong to the respective persistent class but not to a subclass.

If no type identifier is defined, the method can't decide efficiently if an object belongs to a subclass. In this case, it also provides a reference to an object of the persistent class that is managed by the class agent even if the object also belongs to a subclass.

One of the major differences between the three different procedures that enable you to instantiate multiple persistent objects via Object Services lies in the number of required database accesses:

▶ The single instantiation process (refer to Listing 4.1) accesses the database to determine the keys of the persistent objects. Afterwards, the instantiation of each persistent object leads to another database access.

▶ For mass instantiation (refer to Listing 4.2), ideally only two database accesses are necessary to instantiate multiple persistent objects: When you've determined the keys of the persistent objects with the first database access, the Persistence Service can often load all requested persistent objects from the database with only one additional database access. If there are numerous keys, it's possible that the ABAP runtime environment performs multiple database access and only loads a subset of the requested persistent objects from the database with each access.

▶ You can reduce the number of database accesses to a minimum using the Query Service (refer to Listing 4.3). With only one database access, the Query Service passes the filter and sort conditions defined by you to the database system. As a result of this query, the database system returns the persistent attributes for all objects that correspond to this query so that no additional database access are necessary.

Due to the reduced communication requirement between application server and database system, you can further accelerate the instantiation process for persistent objects in many cases if you use the Query Service instead of mass instantiation. For example, the instantiation of 100,000 persistent objects using the Query Service can be twice as fast as with mass instantiation. Here as well, the factor by which the speed differs depends on the system and on the persistent class.

4.4 More Complex Selections Using the Query Service

The simple example from Section 4.3, Simple Selections Using the Query Service, illustrated how you can create a query with a plain filter condition using the Query Service. This section now discusses how you can formulate a more complex filter condition consisting of several individual criteria and define the sort condition.

Filter conditions also allow you to use *query parameters*. Query parameters enable you to create a query object with a filter condition once and then execute this query with different values in the individual criteria of the filter condition. For example, you can create a query object in whose filter condition you can define that you want to instantiate flight plans with a specific departure location and a specific destination location. In the filter condition, you don't specify the concrete airports, but refer to the query parameters first. You can then execute the query created in this way several times and specify through the query parameters which concrete departure location and destination location is supposed to be used for this execution of the query.

4.4.1 Defining Query Parameters

Without you having to make further specifications, each query provides three query parameters, which you can use to formulate filter conditions. These are called PAR1, PAR2, and PAR3. If you want to use more than three query parameters in the filter condition or assign meaningful names to the query parameters, you have the following two options:

▶ You pass the I_PARAMETERS importing parameter to the CREATE_QUERY method when creating the query. To do so, you use a string in which the individual names of the query parameters are separated by a blank. Listing 4.4 shows the definition of two query parameters called PAR_AIRPFROM and PAR_AIRPTO. For this way of defining query parameters, case sensitivity isn't relevant. Irrespective of whether you use only lowercase letters or only uppercase letters to write the names of the parameters, the system creates query parameters with names in uppercase letters.

```
DATA: ri_query_manager    TYPE REF TO if_os_query_manager,
      ri_query            TYPE REF TO if_os_query.

ri_query_manager = cl_os_system=>get_query_manager( ).

* Create a new query and define the names of the parameters
* simultaneously
ri_query =
  ri_query_manager->create_query(
    i_parameters = 'PAR_AIRPFROM PAR_AIRPTO' ).
```

Listing 4.4 Setting the Parameter Names When Creating a Query

▶ Alternatively, you can define the names of the query parameters using a so-called *parameter expression* after you have created the query. For this purpose, you can have the query object provide a reference to an expression factory using the GET_EXPR_FACTORY method. The expression factory provides a method called CREATE_PARAMETERS_EXPR, which creates a parameter expression and returns a reference to the object. You can then successively transfer the names of the query parameters to the APPEND method of the parameter expression with each call of the method. Finally, you pass the complete parameter expression with the names of all query parameters to the SET_PARAMETERS_EXPR method of the query.

When creating parameter expressions, case sensitivity is relevant for the names of the query parameters. You should only use uppercase letters for all parameter names to avoid problems during the execution of the query.

Like Listing 4.4, Listing 4.5 illustrates the described process by means of two parameters called PAR_AIRPFROM and PAR_AIRPTO.

```
DATA: ri_query_manager    TYPE REF TO if_os_query_manager,
      ri_query            TYPE REF TO if_os_query,
      ri_expr_factory     TYPE REF TO if_os_query_expr_factory,
      ri_parameters_expr TYPE REF TO if_os_query_parameters_expr.

* Create a new query
ri_query_manager = cl_os_system=>get_query_manager( ).
ri_query = ri_query_manager->create_query( ).

* Get a reference to the expression factory
ri_expr_factory = ri_query->get_expr_factory( ).

* Create a new parameter expression
ri_parameters_expr = ri_expr_factory->create_parameters_expr( ).

* Define the names of the parameters in the parameter expression
ri_parameters_expr->append( 'PAR_AIRPFROM' ).
ri_parameters_expr->append( 'PAR_AIRPTO' ).

* Assign parameter expression to the query
ri_query->set_parameters_expr( ri_parameters_expr ).
```

Listing 4.5 Setting the Parameter Names Using a Parameter Expression

Defining the parameter names via a parameter expression involves much more effort than defining the names during the creation of the query. Because the expressive power of the two variants is the same, you should always define parameter names during the creation of the query.

The names of the query parameters can consist of the letters A to Z, the numbers 0 to 9, and the underscore. The name must start with a letter. To avoid naming conflicts, the name of a parameter mustn't be identical to the name of an attribute of the persistent class for which you want to instantiate the persistent objects.

You can use the defined parameters for the formulation of the filter condition. When executing the query, you then have to specify a value for any parameter that you used in the filter condition.

4.4.2 Defining the Filter Condition

The filter condition enables you to limit the objects a query is supposed to return via the Query Service. For this purpose, you can — referring to the persistent attributes of the persistent objects — specify criteria that are supposed to be met by any object that the query returns.

You can also execute a query using the Query Service without defining a filter condition. In this case, the query returns references to all persistent objects of the persistent class.

Similarly to parameter names, you have two options for defining filter conditions:

▶ You specify the filter condition in an SQL-similar syntax when creating the query.

▶ You define a so-called filter expression after creating the query.

Defining the Filter Condition During the Creation of the Query

When creating a query using the CREATE_QUERY method, you can work with the I_FILTER parameter to pass a string that contains the filter condition. To formulate filter conditions, you can use a subset of the basic language elements, which also enable you to define a WHERE clause in Open SQL. Also, an additional operator is available, which allows for using references to further persistent objects in conditions.

The relational operators, = (equal), <> (not equal), < (less than), <= (less than or equal), > (greater than), and >= (greater than or equal), enable you to define which values a persistent attribute may adopt so that the result of the query includes the persistent object. You always have to define the name of a persistent attribute on the left side of the relational operator, but the right side can be the name of a persistent attribute, the name of a query parameter, or a value in the form of a literal. Literals with all data types, including numbers, always need to be enclosed in single inverted commas (') in the string that contains the filter condition.

Listing 4.6 shows three possible filter conditions with relational operators:

▶ v_filter_1 selects all flight plans in which a maximum flight time of 120 minutes is specified. Here, as a literal, the maximum flight time is enclosed in inverted commas. When specifying the filter condition as a string literal in the ABAP source code, you have to use two single inverted commas, respectively, so that the string contains an inverted comma at the appropriate position.

▶ v_filter_2 enables you to instantiate all flights that take place on a specific date. For this purpose, you must pass a concrete date value for the default PAR1 query parameter when executing the query.

▶ v_filter_3 compares two persistent attributes. You can use this filter condition to select all flights for which the same number of seats is occupied in the business class and in the first class.

```
DATA: v_filter_1 TYPE string,
      v_filter_2 TYPE string,
      v_filter_3 TYPE string.

v_filter_1 = 'FLTIME <= ''120'''.
v_filter_2 = 'FLDATE = PAR1'.
v_filter_3 = 'SEATSOCC_B = SEATSOCC_F'.
```
Listing 4.6 Filter Conditions with Relational Operators

The LIKE operator enables you to check the value of a persistent attribute against a template. In the template, you can use the underscore (_) if exactly one random character is possible at the corresponding position. If any number of characters can be used here, use the percentage sign (%). You can use the ESCAPE addition to define an escape character. If the selected escape character is used in front of the underscore or the percentage sign, these characters lose their special function. This way, you can express that the actual underscore or percentage sign is required at a specific position also when using the LIKE operator.

Listing 4.7 provides examples of the use of the LIKE operator:

▶ `v_filter_4` searches for all flight customers with email addresses that contain the characters `"@sap."`. The number of additional characters that precede these characters is unlimited, but there can be only two arbitrary characters after these characters.

▶ `v_filter_5` searches for all customers with an email address that contains the name Benjamin followed by an underscore. Because the actual underscore sign is needed here and not the meaning of the underscore as a wildcard for any character, the number sign (#) is defined as the escape character. Written one after the other, the number sign escape character and the underscore effect that the query searches the email address for the underscore and doesn't interpret the underscore as a wildcard for any character.

```
DATA: v_filter_4 TYPE string,
      v_filter_5 TYPE string.

v_filter_4 = 'EMAIL LIKE ''%@sap.__'''.
v_filter_5 = 'EMAIL LIKE ''%Benjamin#_%'' ESCAPE ''#'''.
```

Listing 4.7 Filter Conditions with the LIKE Operator

Null values, that is, fields of a database table that have explicitly been defined as empty, usually don't occur if you work with Object Services in a database table. Only if you've created new fields for a database table that already contains data records or if you write to the database table directly with Open SQL and without Object Services, can it happen that a database table contains a null value — instead of the respective initial value of the data type. To identify this kind of constellation, you can use the IS NULL operator.

In addition to the operators described before, which are also available in Open SQL, you can also work with the EQUALSREF operator in the filter condition of a query when using the Query Service. The EQUALSREF operator enables you to check if a persistent reference refers to the same persistent object as a usual reference to a persistent object in the running application. Before the EQUALSREF operator, you always have to specify the name of a persistent attribute that is defined as a persistent reference in the persistence representation. The name of a parameter must always follow the operator.

You can use the logical operators AND and OR to merge two expressions into a new expression. The logical operator NOT enables you to invert the result of the expression. You can use parentheses to define the sequence in which the system is supposed to evaluate the individual logical operators. In this case, every parenthesis needs to be separated by at least one blank from all other parts of the filter condition.

The query, which you can execute with the filter condition from Listing 4.8, instantiates all flight plans in which a departure airport is in Germany and a destination airport is in the United States or in Japan.

```
DATA: v_filter_6 TYPE string.

v_filter_6 =
  'COUNTRYFROM = ''DE'' AND ' &
  '( COUNTRYTO = ''US'' OR COUNTRYTO = ''JP'' )'.
```

Listing 4.8 Filter Condition with Logical Operators

If you define the filter condition when creating the query, case sensitivity isn't relevant. When executing the query, the system automatically converts the names of parameters and attributes as well as the logical operators to uppercase. Case sensitivity is only important for literals against which you want to check the values of attributes.

Defining the Filter Condition Using a Filter Expression

Similarly to the definition of the names of the used query parameters, you can also use the expression factory to define the filter condition. Here, the expression factory enables you to generate a filter expression, which you finally assign to the query.

The basic idea of this kind of filter condition definition is that you create a tree of objects in which each object represents a part of the filter condition. Every leaf of a tree stands for an individual condition referring to a persistent attribute. The internal nodes link partial conditions by means of logical operators.

Four types of expression objects can be used as the leaves of the tree:

▶ *Operator expressions* enable you to compare a persistent attribute with another persistent attribute, with a parameter, or with a passed value using a relational operator. Here, you can use the same relational operators as for the definition of the filter condition during the creation of the query.

▶ *LIKE expressions* allow you to check a persistent attribute against a template using the LIKE operator.

▶ Checks for the null value are carried out using the *IS NULL expression*. These checks correspond to the use of the IS NULL operator.

▶ Like the EQUALSREF operator, the *reference expression* determines if a persistent reference refers to a persistent object defined by you.

You create all expressions using the corresponding method of the expression factory. Every method provides individual parameters that you can use to transfer specifications such as the persistent attribute that is supposed to be compared, the relational operator, or the comparison value. In most of the methods, an importing parameter called I_IDX is defined. If you want to refer to a parameter of the query in an expression, use this importing parameter to specify the index of the query parameter. The index of the query parameter can be derived from the sequence in which you have defined the names of the query parameters. The first query parameter is assigned index 1; the Query Service numbers all other parameters in ascending order.

For several methods, you can either pass a value that the Query Service automatically encloses in inverted commas in the database query, or you can pass a value that already contains the required inverted commas. The names of the importing parameters for which you have to pass values including the inverted commas end with the _W_QUOTES (with quotes) suffix. If in doubt, you should always use the alternative importing parameter without the _W_QUOTES suffix.

AND and OR expressions enable you to link two expressions with a logical "and" or with a logical "or". Because the linked expressions can be both individual expressions and a tree of already-created links of several expressions, you can use these expressions to create trees of any size. When creating a NOT expression, you only transfer a single expression. The NOT expression then negates this expression.

Figure 4.1 and Listing 4.9 show the same filter condition, which was already formulated in Listing 4.8. The UML object diagram in Figure 4.1 illustrates the objects the filter condition consists of. There is one object for each subexpression the filter condition contains. The tree as a whole describes the filter condition that states that the departure airport is supposed to be in Germany and the destination airport in the United States or in Japan.

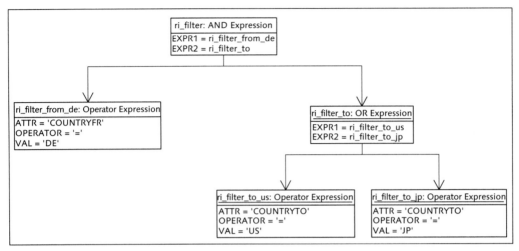

Figure 4.1   Object Diagram of a Filter Expression

```
DATA:  rf_ca_spfli        TYPE REF TO /iot/ca_spfli,
       ri_query_manager   TYPE REF TO if_os_query_manager,
       ri_query           TYPE REF TO if_os_query,
       ri_expr_factory    TYPE REF TO if_os_query_expr_factory,
       ri_filter_from_de  TYPE REF TO if_os_query_filter_expr,
       ri_filter_to_us    TYPE REF TO if_os_query_filter_expr,
       ri_filter_to_jp    TYPE REF TO if_os_query_filter_expr,
       ri_filter_to       TYPE REF TO if_os_query_filter_expr,
       ri_filter          TYPE REF TO if_os_query_filter_expr,
       ta_ro_spfli        TYPE osreftab.

ri_query_manager = cl_os_system=>get_query_manager( ).
rf_ca_spfli = /iot/ca_spfli=>agent.

* Create query
ri_query = ri_query_manager->create_query( ).

* Get reference to expression factory
ri_expr_factory = ri_query->get_expr_factory( ).

* Create filter expression: departure country Germany
ri_filter_from_de =
  ri_expr_factory->create_operator_expr(
    i_attr1    = 'COUNTRYFR'
    i_operator = '='
    i_val      = 'DE' ).
```

```
* Create filter expression: destination country USA
ri_filter_to_us =
  ri_expr_factory->create_operator_expr(
    i_attr1   = 'COUNTRYTO'
    i_operator = '='
    i_val     = 'US' ).

* Create filter expression: destination country Japan
ri_filter_to_jp =
  ri_expr_factory->create_operator_expr(
    i_attr1   = 'COUNTRYTO'
    i_operator = '='
    i_val     = 'JP' ).

* Create filter expression: "or" link between destination
* countries
ri_filter_to =
  ri_expr_factory->create_or_expr(
    i_expr1 = ri_filter_to_us
    i_expr2 = ri_filter_to_jp ).

* Create filter expression: "and" link between departure
* country and the two alternative destination countries
ri_filter =
  ri_expr_factory->create_and_expr(
    i_expr1 = ri_filter_from_de
    i_expr2 = ri_filter_to ).

* Assign complete filter expression to query
ri_query->set_filter_expr( ri_filter ).

* Execute query
ta_ro_spfli =
  rf_ca_spfli->if_os_ca_persistency~get_persistent_by_query(
    ri_query ).
```

Listing 4.9 Definition and Use of a Filter Expression

To create the individual objects that are supposed to form the tree with the filter condition, you first require a reference to the expression factory again. In the expression factory, you call the respective methods, one after the other, for creating the specific expression objects.

For more complex filter conditions that consist of multiple objects (see Listing 4.9), you have to create the tree according to the bottom-up approach: You first generate the tree's leaves, that is, the conditions that directly refer to a persistent attribute. The names of the attributes must be transferred in uppercase characters only. Then, you create the internal nodes, which link the already-existing objects by using the logical operators AND, OR, and NOT. Finally, you assign the query as a filter condition to the root of the tree (in Figure 4.1, the highest-level object) via its SET_FILTER_EXPR method. Because only the root is connected to all parts of the tree via the references, it's the only object from which the Query Service can derive the complete filter condition.

Comparing the Two Variants for the Definition of the Filter Condition

The expressive power of the two variants for the definition of filter conditions is the same; that is, you could also use the respective other variant to formulate any filter condition that you can create using one of the two variants. However, you should create filter conditions during the creation of the query, because — compared to using a filter expression — this can be implemented with less effort, and the source code is more legible. It only makes sense to use the filter expression if you want to compose the filter condition dynamically at runtime.

4.4.3   Defining the Sort Condition

The sort condition of a query enables you to specify in which sequence the persistent objects are supposed to be sorted in the result table after the query has been executed. For this purpose, you can refer to one or several persistent attributes and define for each attribute whether the sorting is supposed to be done in ascending or descending order.

If you don't define a sort condition, Object Services return the persistent objects in the sequence in which the database system returned the corresponding data records. In many cases, the data records are sorted in ascending order according to the primary key of the database table. However, because you can't be sure that every system has this behavior, you should always explicitly specify the sort condition if how the persistent objects are sorted is relevant for your application.

You can define the sort condition in two ways:

▶ You pass the I_ORDERING parameter to the CREATE_QUERY method during the creation of the query.

▶ You define a sort expression via the expression factory and pass it to the SET_ORDERING_EXPR method of the query.

Defining the Sort Condition During the Creation of the Query

To the I_ORDERING parameter of the CREATE_QUERY method, you have to transfer a string that contains the name of a persistent attribute followed by the ASCENDING (sorted in ascending order) or DESCENDING (sorted in descending order) keyword. The persistent attributes and the keywords for the sorting sequence must be separated by blanks, respectively. For this variant, case sensitivity isn't relevant.

The sequence in which you specify multiple persistent attributes determines the sequence in which the system sorts the individual attributes: The system initially sorts the persistent object by the first specified persistent attribute. If required and defined, it then sorts all other persistent attributes.

Listing 4.10 shows an example of a sort condition with two persistent attributes. The query that is created in the listing instantiates flights from the flight data model. Object Services sort the flights in descending order according to the flight date. Consequently, earlier flights are listed higher in the result table than later flights. The query sorts all flights on the same date in descending order according to the SEATSMAX attribute. So, it first returns the flights with the most seats in the economy class and lastly the flights with the lowest capacity.

```
ri_query =
  ri_query_manager->create_query(
    i_ordering = 'FLDATE ASCENDING SEATSMAX DESCENDING' ).
```

Listing 4.10 Defining the Sort Condition During the Creation of the Query

Defining the Sort Condition Using a Sort Expression

Similar to parameter expressions and filter expressions, you can also create a query, in which no sort condition is defined, and then use the expression factory to create a *sort expression*.

You can call two methods on a sort expression: a method for adding a persistent attribute according to which the sorting is to be done in ascending order (APPEND_

ASCENDING), and a method for adding a persistent attribute according to which the sorting is to be done in descending order (APPEND_DESCENDING). You always have to transfer the name of the persistent attribute in uppercase letters. Here, the sequence in which you add the persistent attributes also determines the sequence in which the persistent attributes will be used to determine the order of the persistent objects.

Listing 4.11 defines the same sort condition as Listing 4.10 using a sort expression. For this purpose, the CREATE_ORDERING_EXPR method of the expression factory is called. It creates a sort expression. The respective methods for adding persistent attributes by which the persistent objects will be sorted in descending and ascending order then are called on the sort expression. Object Services are supposed to sort the query result based on these attributes. Finally, the sort expression is assigned to the query.

```
DATA: ri_query_manager TYPE REF TO if_os_query_manager,
      ri_query         TYPE REF TO if_os_query,
      ri_expr_factory  TYPE REF TO if_os_query_expr_factory,
      ri_ordering_expr TYPE REF TO if_os_query_ordering_expr.

ri_query_manager = cl_os_system=>get_query_manager( ).

* Create query
ri_query = ri_query_manager->create_query( ).

* Get reference to expression factory
ri_expr_factory = ri_query->get_expr_factory( ).

* Create sort expression
ri_ordering_expr = ri_expr_factory->create_ordering_expr( ).

* Define persistent attributes by which the objects are
* sorted:
* - Ascending by flight date
* - Descending by maximum seating in economy class
ri_ordering_expr->append_ascending( 'FLDATE' ).
ri_ordering_expr->append_descending( 'SEATSMAX' ).

* Assign sort expression to query
ri_query->set_ordering_expr( ri_ordering_expr ).
```

Listing 4.11 Defining the Sort Condition Using a Sort Expression

Comparing the Two Variants for the Definition of the Sort Condition

The expressive power of the two variants for the definition of the sort condition is identical, too. In general, you can always use both variants to formulate any kind of sort condition. However, the variant for defining the sort condition during the creation of the query is usually more comfortable and less complex, particularly for constant sort conditions. The variant for the definition via a sort expression might be more useful if you want to create the sort condition dynamically at runtime.

4.4.4 Passing Concrete Values for Query Parameters

For all query parameters that you have defined and actually used in the filter condition, you have to transfer the concrete value with which you want to execute the query when calling the query. Only if you haven't made any reference to a query parameter in the filter condition, can you execute a query without having to specify values for query parameters.

There are two options for passing parameter values, namely, a simplified option with limited functions, and an option for more complex queries:

▸ If you use three parameters at the most and don't evaluate persistent references in the query, you can pass the values of the query parameters to the IF_OS_ CA_PERSISTENCY~GET_PERSISTENT_BY_QUERY method using the I_PAR1 to I_PAR3 importing parameters.

▸ You can transfer an internal table with data references to the IF_OS_CA_ PERSISTENCY~GET_PERSISTENT_BY_QUERY method in any case, that is, irrespective of the number of the parameters and also if you work with persistent references.

Passing Individual Parameters: I_PAR1 to I_PAR3

The parameter interface of the IF_OS_CA_PERSISTENCY~GET_PERSISTENT_BY_QUERY method contains three optional importing parameters called I_PAR1, I_PAR2, and I_PAR3. You can use these parameters to transfer concrete values for the parameters used. Because the importing parameters are defined with the ANY type, you can pass any value of an elementary type to them. Passing a reference to a persistent object, in contrast, isn't possible.

Listing 4.12 instantiates all flights that take place in October 2009. Here, the filter condition refers to the default parameters, PAR1 and PAR2. The concrete values

(October 01 and October 31, 2009, in this case) aren't passed until the query is being executed. Without having to create a new query object, you can execute the query any number of times and always request flights from a different date interval.

```
DATA: ri_query_manager TYPE REF TO if_os_query_manager,
      ri_query           TYPE REF TO if_os_query,
      ta_ro_flights      TYPE osreftab,
      rf_ca_sflight      TYPE REF TO /iot/ca_sflight.

rf_ca_sflight = /iot/ca_sflight=>agent.
ri_query_manager = cl_os_system=>get_query_manager( ).

* Create query
ri_query =
  ri_query_manager->create_query(
    i_filter = 'FLDATE >= PAR1 AND FLDATE <= PAR2' ).

* Execute query
ta_ro_flights =
  rf_ca_sflight->if_os_ca_persistency~get_persistent_by_query(
    i_query = ri_query
    i_par1  = '20091001'
    i_par2  = '20091031' ).
```

Listing 4.12 Query Passing Individual Parameters

To use the I_PAR1 to I_PAR3 importing parameters when executing a query, you don't necessarily have to work with query parameters called PAR1 to PAR3. The I_PAR1 to I_PAR3 importing parameters, respectively, refer to the first, second, and third defined query parameter, irrespective of its name. For example, if you have defined two query parameters with user-defined names, you can assign concrete values to them using the I_PAR1 and I_PAR2 importing parameters when executing the query.

Passing an Internal Table Using Query Parameters: I_PARAMETER_TAB

The I_PARAMETER_TAB importing parameter provides an alternative for passing values for query parameters. This importing parameter enables you to transfer an internal table in which each line contains a data reference to the value to which you want to pass the query parameter. A data reference allows for referring to a variable, a constant, a literal of an elementary type, or a reference to an object.

This variant for passing query parameters also doesn't require a direct reference to the names of the query parameter. The sequence in which you defined the names of the query parameters also determines the sequence you have to use for the data references in the internal table: The data reference to the value for the first defined query parameter needs to be specified in the first line, the data reference to the value for the next defined parameter in the second line, and so on.

Listing 4.13 illustrates how you can populate an internal table with data references and then use this table to execute a query.

```
DATA: dr_rf_airport     TYPE REF TO data,
      rf_ca_airport     TYPE REF TO /iot/ca_sairport,
      rf_ca_counter     TYPE REF TO /iot/ca_scounter,
      rf_airport        TYPE REF TO /iot/cl_sairport,
      ri_query_manager  TYPE REF TO if_os_query_manager,
      ri_query          TYPE REF TO if_os_query,
      ta_parameters     TYPE osdreftab,
      ta_ro_counters    TYPE osreftab.

rf_ca_airport = /iot/ca_sairport=>agent.
rf_ca_counter = /iot/ca_scounter=>agent.
ri_query_manager = cl_os_system=>get_query_manager( ).

* Create query
ri_query =
  ri_query_manager->create_query(
    i_filter = 'RF_AIRPORT EQUALSREF PAR1').

* Instantiate Frankfurt Airport
rf_airport = rf_ca_airport->get_persistent( i_id = 'FRA' ).

* Append airport object data reference to parameter
* table
GET REFERENCE OF rf_airport INTO dr_rf_airport.
APPEND dr_rf_airport TO ta_parameters.

* Execute query
ta_ro_counters =
  rf_ca_counter->if_os_ca_persistency~get_persistent_by_query(
    i_query         = ri_query
    i_parameter_tab = ta_parameters ).
```

Listing 4.13 Query with Transfer of an Internal Table with Parameters

The filter condition of the query contains the EQUALSREF operator, that is, a condition referring to a persistent reference. In this case, the query is supposed to determine all airline sales counters at a specific airport. For this purpose, the filter condition refers to the RF_AIRPORT attribute. For each counter, this attribute contains a persistent reference to the airport at which the counter is located.

To use a condition with a persistent reference in a query, you need a reference to an already-instantiated persistent object. Consequently, the corresponding persistent object is instantiated to determine the counters at Frankfurt Airport.

The GET REFERENCE OF statement generates a data reference, which you require for the internal table with the values of the query parameters. If you apply this to the reference to a persistent object, you receive a two-level reference, that is, a data reference to a reference to a persistent object in this case. Then, you have to append this data reference to the internal table that contains the values of the query parameters before passing the table to the I_PARAMETER_TAB importing parameter during the execution of the query.

Comparing the Two Variants for Passing Concrete Values for Query Parameters

It's considerably easier to pass individual parameters, I_PAR1 to I_PAR3, than the internal table with the I_PARAMETER_TAB parameters. You should therefore only use the internal table if a transfer of individual parameters is out of question, that is, if more than three parameters are used or a persistent reference is referenced.

4.5   Comparing the Query Service and Open SQL

You can benefit from two advantages if you work with a simple query using the Query Service to instantiate persistent objects instead of determining the keys of persistent objects with a SELECT query in Open SQL and then loading them: The ABAP source code that you need to implement is more compact, and the whole process requires only one database access, which reduces the load on the application server and database system as well as the communication between them. This, in turn, may make your application significantly faster.

If you use the Query Service, the keys of the objects on the application server aren't known before the objects are instantiated. Consequently, you can't work with the keys of the objects before the instantiation. As further described in Chapter 8,

Integration of the SAP Lock Concept and Object Services, this is a disadvantage, particularly in the SAP Lock Concept context.

The expressive power of the queries using the Query Service and the expressive power of the SELECT queries in Open SQL differ considerably. The Query Service always instantiates complete persistent objects. Therefore, SELECT clauses for the specification of the fields that are supposed to be loaded, equivalents to the GROUP BY and HAVING clauses, and aggregate functions don't exist. The functional scope of the Query Service also doesn't include subqueries or joins for arbitrary tables.

A FROM clause isn't required if you work with the Query Service because the Query Service uses the information from the persistence representation, which contains the underlying database tables. Concerning persistent references, the Query Service also uses already-existing information in the system and thus reduces the development work compared to an equivalent query in Open SQL.

Open SQL is an integral part of the ABAP programming language. As a result, the system can check the syntax of queries in Open SQL already during the development time if they don't contain dynamic components. The syntactic correctness of a filter condition of a query that was implemented using the Query Service, in contrast, can be checked by the system at runtime only.

Both the selection via the Query Service and the selection with Open SQL are solely based on the database's data. If you've created, changed, or deleted persistent objects in the running program, and you don't want to transfer these changes to the database yet, the result of the selection is still based on the original state without considering the changes. The next section describes how you can use the functions of the class agents to have the selections consider changes that you've made to persistent objects only in the memory of the running application.

4.6   Handling Newly Created and Changed Objects

Each class agent of a persistent class contains methods that you can respectively use to determine the persistent objects of the class that have a certain management state. This way, you can among other things determine all persistent objects of the class that you've created, changed, or deleted in the current top-level transaction.

The methods are defined in the IF_OS_CA_INSTANCE interface. Their respective names begin with the GET_ prefix, which is then, except for one exception, followed by the name of the corresponding management state. This exception is the GET_CREATED method, which determines the persistent objects in the NEW management state.

The respective methods only provide objects that belong to the respective persistent class that the class agent manages. The methods don't return objects that are included in the management of a class agent of a subclass or superclass.

Listing 4.14 shows how you can adapt the result of a query in such a way that it also considers newly created objects. The query determines all flights that take place on the current date. When the query has been executed, the GET_CREATED method determines all references to newly created objects. In a LOOP loop, it's then manually checked for every newly created flight if it meets the filter condition. If so, the GET_FLDATE access method reads the flight date and compares it to the current date. If the flight date is identical to the current date, the newly created flight is added to the internal table that contains all previously determined flights on the current date.

```
DATA: rf_ca_sflight     TYPE REF TO /iot/ca_sflight,
      rf_sflight        TYPE REF TO /iot/cl_sflight,
      ri_query_manager  TYPE REF TO if_os_query_manager,
      ri_query          TYPE REF TO if_os_query,
      ro_sflight        TYPE REF TO object,
      ta_ro_sflights    TYPE osreftab,
      ta_ro_created     TYPE osreftab.

rf_ca_sflight = /iot/ca_sflight=>agent.
ri_query_manager = cl_os_system=>get_query_manager( ).

* Create query
ri_query =
  ri_query_manager->create_query(
    i_filter = 'FLDATE = PAR1' ).

* Execute query
ta_ro_sflights =
  rf_ca_sflight->if_os_ca_persistency~get_persistent_by_query(
    i_query = ri_query
    i_par1  = sy-datum ).

* Determine newly created persistent objects
ta_ro_created =
  rf_ca_sflight->if_os_ca_instance~get_created( ).
```

```
* Check every newly created persistent object against
* filter condition
LOOP AT ta_ro_created INTO ro_sflight.
* Typecast: OBJECT -> /IOT/CL_SFLIGHT
  rf_sflight ?= ro_sflight.

  IF rf_sflight->get_fldate( ) = sy-datum.
* Object corresponds to filter condition
* -> Add to result table
    APPEND rf_sflight TO ta_ro_sflights.
  ENDIF.
ENDLOOP.
```

Listing 4.14 Manual Consideration of Newly Created Objects

To also include changed objects in a selection, you have to consider two constellations:

▶ Owing to the change, a persistent object can correspond to the filter condition while the present state in the database doesn't meet the filter condition yet. Consider this case in the same way as in Listing 4.14 and determine the changed objects using the GET_CHANGED method. In addition, remember that a changed object might have already met the filter condition previously. You therefore need to ensure that the result table doesn't add an already-contained object again.

▶ In the reverse case, the present state in the database meets the filter condition, but the changed objects in the memory of the running application no longer meets the condition. To remove such objects from the query's result, you should initially check the management state of any determined object (IF_OS_CA_INSTANCE~GET_STATUS method, see Section 3.4, Management States of Persistent Objects, in Chapter 3). You have to check all objects in the CHANGED management state manually against the filter condition using the access methods. If an object no longer meets the filter condition, remove it from the result.

Object Services automatically consider objects that were deleted in the running program to a certain degree. If you try to use mass instantiation or a query via the Query Service to instantiate an object that has already been deleted in the running program, the system raises an exception of the CX_OS_OBJECT_NOT_FOUND class. As a result, the deleted object automatically isn't instantiated. If the exception occurs, the instantiation of further objects is also terminated.

That means you don't receive a result that doesn't include the deleted objects, you receive no result at all. To still instantiate all objects that haven't been deleted — despite existing deleted objects — you can use an approach as implemented in Listing 4.1: Determine the keys of the objects by means of a query in Open SQL and then instantiate them separately. This way, you only include the persistent objects in the result during whose instantiation no exception of the CX_OS_OBJECT_ NOT_FOUND class occurs.

As of EhP2 for Release 7.0 of SAP NetWeaver AS ABAP, you can also control the Query Service's behavior regarding deleted objects. If you pass the IGNORE_DELETED option when executing a query, the Query Service doesn't raise an exception when it detects deleted objects. Instead, the query provides a result that doesn't include the deleted objects.

In more complex applications that change a lot of persistent objects during a top-level transaction, you usually have to consider newly created and changed objects in the selection of persistent objects. If your application allows for the execution of queries when you've already changed persistent objects in the current top-level transaction, the queries don't provide a result that is correct with regard to content if newly created and changed objects aren't considered. However, if your application is structured in such a way that every top-level transaction begins with loading all involved objects first and then makes all changes, special handling for newly created and changed objects isn't required in the selection.

4.7   Summary

This chapter described how you can select persistent objects according to user-defined criteria. In some cases, you can use the Object Services Query Service for this purpose. You also learned in which cases it's necessary and useful to use Open SQL statements that have already been available in classic ABAP instead of the Query Service.

This chapter also provided a first proposal for an enhancement of the Object Services functionality: considering objects in the memory for selections. The next chapter explains the internal functioning of Object Services and thus introduces the basic principles of the additional enhancements, which are discussed in Chapters 6 to 8.

The previous chapters detailed the functions provided by Object Services in every SAP NetWeaver AS ABAP. This chapter describes how the functions of Object Services are implemented.

5 Internal Structure and Functioning of Object Services

In principle, Object Services can also be used as a black box, that is, without knowledge of the internal processes. However, knowledge about the internal functioning of Object Services is helpful if you're looking for an error in your program or you're considering enhancing the functions of Object Services with your own developments. For this reason, this chapter outlines the internal structure and the functioning of the Persistence Service and the Transaction Service; you also learn about further functions that you can call via the CL_OS_SYSTEM class.

5.1 Persistence Service

The following sections detail the implementation of the Persistence Service. This includes a description of the implementation of class agents, the presentation of the Instance Manager and the Persistency Manager, as well as illustrations of the automatic source code generation and garbage collection.

5.1.1 Class Agent and Base Agent

The implementation of a class agent consists of three classes: a universal superclass of all class agents, a subclass with automatically generated specializations for the respective persistent class, and the actual class agent class in which you can implement your own enhancements.

The class diagram in Figure 5.1 shows this inheritance hierarchy using the example of the persistent class /IOT/CL_SFLIGHT. The general part, which forms the basis for all class agents of persistent classes, is implemented in the abstract class,

CL_OS_CA_COMMON. This class implements that part of the persistent object management that doesn't depend on the persistence representation of a concrete class. Among other things, it's programmed here where the class agent stores the management state of every persistent object, and in which situations transitions take place from one management state of a persistent object to another. The methods for determining all managed objects that are in a specific management state are also implemented here. Also, the CL_OS_CA_COMMON class contains universal implementations of methods that you can use to instruct the Persistence Service to reload an object with the next access to the database or remove it from the management.

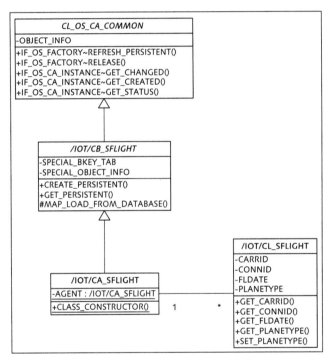

Figure 5.1 Class Diagram with a Class Agent and the Corresponding Persistent Class

For each concrete persistent class you create, the Persistence Service generates two additional classes: the already-known class agent with the CA abbreviation in the name, and the *base agent* with the CB abbreviation in the name. The abstract class of the base agent includes all functions that the Persistence Service adapts to the specifications of the persistence representation of the corresponding persistent class. Here, for example, you can find the implementations of the methods for creating and instantiating objects, which were presented in Chapter 2, Reading Persistent Objects, and Chapter 3, Creating and Changing Persistent Objects.

The class of the base agent also includes implementations of many other methods with the Protected visibility. These are called by other methods of the same class. However, they aren't available outside the class agent. For example, these methods comprise the MAP_LOAD_FROM_DATABASE method that contains an Open SQL statement for loading persistent objects from the database.

The Persistence Service creates the actual class agent class as a subclass of the base agent and consequently as a subclass of CL_OS_CA_COMMON. The automatically generated ABAP source code of the class agent class itself only consists of the implementation of the singleton design pattern. This includes the static attribute, AGENT, and the class constructor, which generates an object of the class when the class is accessed for the first time and stores a reference to this object in the AGENT attribute.

Each class agent contains various attributes that the agent uses to manage the persistent objects and the changes to these objects. One of the most important attributes of the class agent is the internal table OBJECT_INFO. Table 5.1 provides a list of the most important fields of this internal table.

Field	Description
OBJECT_ID	Object ID of the persistent object in the running internal session
	It is identical to the object ID that the ABAP Debugger displays for every object. It is a consecutively assigned identifier that uniquely identifies an object in the running internal session. Don't confuse it with the globally valid instance GUID of the object.
OBJECT_IREF	Reference to the persistent object
	The reference is set only if the persistent object isn't in the NOT LOADED management state. The garbage collection can therefore release objects in the NOT LOADED management state (see Section 5.1.5, Garbage Collection in ABAP Objects).
PM_STATUS	Management state of the persistent object (see Section 3.4, Management States of Persistent Objects, in Chapter 3)

Table 5.1 Important Fields of the OBJECT_INFO Internal Table

Field	Description
PM_DBSTATUS	Database status of the persistent object The database status can have the following values: ▶ OSCON_DBSTATUS_UNKNOWN (0): It's unknown whether the persistent object already exists in the database. ▶ OSCON_DBSTATUS_EXISTING (1): The persistent object already exists in the database. ▶ OSCON_DBSTATUS_NOT_EXISTING (2): The persistent object has just been created or is transient and therefore doesn't exist in the database.

Table 5.1 Important Fields of the OBJECT_INFO Internal Table (Cont.)

Figure 5.2 shows sample content of the OBJECT_INFO internal table of the class agent of a persistent class with flights from the flight data model. Nine flights have been instantiated in the running program. All objects are therefore in the LOADED management state (value 2 in the PM_STATUS field) and in the OSCON_DBSTATUS_EXISTING database status (value 1 in the PM_DBSTATUS field).

	Tables	Table Contents			
Table		/IOT/CA_SFLIGHT=>AGENT->OBJECT			
Table Type		Sorted Table[9x16(52)]			
	Line	OBJECT_ID[...	OBJECT_IREF[Reference]	PM_STATUS[I(4)]	PM_DBSTATUS[I(4)]
	1	22	->{O:22*\CLASS=/IOT/CL_SFLIGHT}	2	1
	2	24	->{O:24*\CLASS=/IOT/CL_SFLIGHT}	2	1
	3	26	->{O:26*\CLASS=/IOT/CL_SFLIGHT}	2	1
	4	28	->{O:28*\CLASS=/IOT/CL_SFLIGHT}	2	1
	5	30	->{O:30*\CLASS=/IOT/CL_SFLIGHT}	2	1
	6	32	->{O:32*\CLASS=/IOT/CL_SFLIGHT}	2	1
	7	34	->{O:34*\CLASS=/IOT/CL_SFLIGHT}	2	1
	8	36	->{O:36*\CLASS=/IOT/CL_SFLIGHT}	2	1
	9	38	->{O:38*\CLASS=/IOT/CL_SFLIGHT}	2	1

Figure 5.2 Excerpt of the OBJECT_INFO Internal Table in the ABAP Debugger

The OBJECT_INFO internal table that is defined in the superclass of all class agents, CL_OS_CA_COMMON, only contains general fields; the class of the base agent, however, adds additional internal tables that also contain the concrete business key or the instance GUID of the objects of the persistent class.

For this purpose, two or three internal tables called SPECIAL_OBJECT_INFO, SPE-CIAL_BKEY_TAB, and SPECIAL_OID_TAB exist that depend on the keys that you've defined in the persistence representation. All tables respectively contain a column with the object ID and, if available, a column with the business key and the instance GUID of the managed persistent objects.

The SPECIAL_OBJECT_INFO internal table is defined in every class agent. It's sorted by the object ID and — provided that you know the object ID — enables you to efficiently determine the business key or the instance GUID of a persistent object. If a business key is defined in the persistence representation, the class agent contains the SPECIAL_BKEY_TAB internal table, which is sorted by the business key. Similarly, if the instance GUID is available, the SPECIAL_OID_TAB internal table exists, which is sorted by the instance GUID. For example, if the business key or instance GUID is known, the two tables enable you to efficiently determine the object ID, which you can then use to read the management state from the OBJECT_INFO internal table, which is sorted by the object ID.

A variety of types, which the class agents solely use internally, is defined both in the general superclass of the CL_OS_CA_COMMON class agents and in the classes of the base agents. However, you come across the structured type, TYP_BUSINESS_KEY, if you instantiate or create persistent objects via the business key (see Section 2.2, Instantiating Persistent Objects, in Chapter 2; Section 3.1, Creating Persistent Objects, in Chapter 3; and Section 4.2, Mass Instantiation, in Chapter 4).

The methods, IF_OS_CA_PERSISTENCY~GET_PERSISTENT_BY_KEY, IF_OS_CA_PERSISTENCY~GET_PERSISTENT_BY_KEY_TAB, and IF_OS_FACTORY~CREATE_PERSIS-TENT_BY_KEY, each expect the transfer of the business key in the form of a structure in which the individual fields are sorted alphabetically by the name of the corresponding attributes. By means of the TYP_BUSINESS_KEY internal type, you can manually verify which fields of what type in which sequence the transferred structure must have. Unfortunately, a direct reference to the TYP_BUSINESS_KEY type isn't possible offhand outside the class agent.

5.1.2 Instance Manager and Persistency Manager

Each class agent of a persistent class contains methods that you can use to instantiate persistent objects, determine the management state of a persistent object, or determine all objects in a specific management state. These methods are each designed to work with the objects of a single persistent class. You can use the

Instance Manager and the Persistency Manager to carry out the same tasks for objects of persistent classes without having to access a reference to the class agent of each individual persistent class that participates.

Like for the Transaction Manager and the Query Manager, the CL_OS_SYSTEM class also includes a static method that provides a reference to the respective manager, i.e. to the Instance Manager and the Persistency Manager.

The Instance Manager implements the IF_OS_INSTANCE_MANAGER interface that contains the same methods with the same parameters as the IF_OS_CA_INSTANCE interface that every class agent implements. The methods enable you to determine all persistent objects in a specific management state irrespective of the persistent class to which they belong. Compared to the class agent, only a method for determining all transient objects (GET_TRANSIENT) isn't available in the Instance Manager. The Instance Manager also contains a method for determining the management state of a persistent object of any class (GET_STATUS).

Listing 5.1 shows how you can use the Instance Manager to determine all persistent objects in the LOADED management state irrespective of the persistent class to which they belong. If you've processed flights and customers in your application, the TA_RO_LOADED_OBJECTS internal table will contain references to flights and customers after you've called the GET_LOADED method.

```
DATA: ri_instance_manager  TYPE REF TO if_os_instance_manager,
      ta_ro_loaded_objects TYPE osreftab.

* Get a reference to the Instance Manager
ri_instance_manager = cl_os_system=>get_instance_manager( ).

* Determine all persistent objects in the management state
* LOADED
ta_ro_loaded_objects = ri_instance_manager->get_loaded( ).
```
Listing 5.1 Determining All Persistent Objects in the LOADED Management State

With the Persistency Manager, you can instantiate objects individually, via tables with keys, or via a query with the Query Service without keeping a reference to the class agent. You must respectively specify for which persistent class you want to instantiate the persistent objects.

Instead of a reference to a class agent, you must transfer either the class GUID of the persistent class or the name of the persistent class to the Persistency Manager. When you transfer the name of the persistent class, you must note that the method expects the class name packed in a structure of the SEOCLSKEY type. This structure only contains a single component called CLSNAME to which you must assign the class name in capital letters.

Similar to Listing 4.3 in Chapter 4, Listing 5.2 shows how you instantiate all flights for the current date via a query in the Query Service. In this listing, the GET_PER-SISTENT_BY_QUERY method is called via the Persistency Manager instead of via the class agent of the flight class.

```
DATA:
  ri_persistency_manager  TYPE REF TO if_os_persistency_manager,
  ri_query_manager        TYPE REF TO if_os_query_manager,
  ri_query                TYPE REF TO if_os_query,
  st_class_key            TYPE seoclskey,
  ta_ro_flights           TYPE osreftab.

* Get references to the Persistency Manager and
* the Query Manager
ri_persistency_manager =
  cl_os_system=>get_persistency_manager( ).
ri_query_manager = cl_os_system=>get_query_manager( ).

* Formulate a filter condition and create a query
ri_query =
  ri_query_manager->create_query(
    i_filter = 'FLDATE = PAR1' ).

* Write the name of the persistent class into a structure
st_class_key-clsname = '/IOT/CL_SFLIGHT'.

* Execute query
ta_ro_flights =
  ri_persistency_manager->get_persistent_by_query(
    i_class_name = st_class_key
    i_query      = ri_query
    i_par1       = sy-datum ).
```

Listing 5.2 Instantiating All Flights on the Current Date Using the Persistency Manager

5.1.3 Database Tables with Information on the Persistence Representation

The Persistence Service stores the persistence representation for persistent classes in two database tables. Don't make changes to the content of these database tables because they are only intended for internal use by the runtime environment of SAP NetWeaver AS ABAP. However, you can extract information about the usage of the Persistence Service in your system through read access to this database tables.

For each concrete persistent class, the SEOMAPCLS database table includes information on the database tables the persistence representation uses. Additionally, the generator settings for the persistence representation are stored here.

You can use the SEOMAPATT database table to determine which persistent attributes are assigned to which fields in the database. For a persistent attribute, each data record of the table provides information on the field or — for persistent references — the fields of a database table to which the attribute is assigned. Also, the FIELDTYPE field contains the assignment type of the assignment between the attribute and the field. For example, you can determine in which persistent classes of the system an instance GUID is defined or which classes contain persistent references.

5.1.4 Automatic Source Code Generation

The settings for the persistence representation that are stored in the database form the basis on which the Persistence Service automatically generates ABAP source code. The automatically generated ABAP source code includes the following:

- Many components of the persistent classes itself, such as the access methods for the attributes (GET_ and SET_) and the implementation of the IF_OS_STATE interface
- The entire class of the base agent with all methods, types, attributes, and so on
- In the class of the class agent, the definition as subclass of the class of the base agent, the static attribute AGENT, and the class constructor

You trigger the generation of the source code implicitly in certain actions. You also have the option to explicitly request the Persistence Service to generate the source code again. The Persistence Service generates the source code of the persistent class or the base agent or class agent in the following situations:

▶ When you create or activate a persistent class for the first time, the Persistence Service implements the `IF_OS_STATE` interface in the persistent class. Moreover, it creates the classes of the base agent and the class agent and generates their methods, types, and attributes, provided that this is possible without specifying the persistence representation.

▶ If you define the persistence representation for the first time or edit it at a later point in time, the Persistence Service adjusts the persistent class and the class of the base agent to the new persistence representation. Changes to the generator settings in the persistence representation dialog also trigger the automatic source code generation.

▶ Your actions outside the dialog for persistence representation can also have the result that the Persistence Service generates source code. For example, when you create a transient attribute, the Persistence Service automatically creates access methods for the attribute.

▶ The Persistence Service usually triggers the automatic source code generation automatically if you make changes to the persistent class or its persistence representation. But it can sometimes happen that the Persistence Service doesn't automatically adjust the class agent of the persistent class after you've made changes. This condition typically manifests itself in the form of a syntax error when you activate a class agent or a persistent class. In this case, you can — if you're in the display mode in the persistence representation dialog — trigger the new generation of the class agent via the UTILITIES • GENERATE • CLASS AGENT • CLASS menu path. If subclasses exist for the processed persistent class, you can use the SUBORDINATE CLASSES menu item of the same menu path to generate class agents of all subclasses again.

The source code generators of the Persistence Service are also written in ABAP. Therefore, the ABAP source code of the generators is also available in every SAP NetWeaver AS ABAP. To get detailed information on the generation process, you can analyze the components of the `SOS_MAPPING` package.

You shouldn't directly edit most of the automatically generated methods afterwards to enhance or change their functionality. Because the Persistence Service resets these methods to the original state with the next source code generation run, you would lose all changes you implemented yourself. Therefore, some automatically generated methods include the following note in their comment header: `GENERATED: Do not modify`.

Some generated methods, however, are designed in such a way that you can modify them directly. These methods include the following note in the comment header: Modify if you like. These methods include the IF_OS_STATE~INIT method in every persistent class. The Persistence Service calls this method after it has loaded the persistent attributes of the persistent object, that is, when you create and instantiate a persistent object as well as when you load the persistent attributes for an object in the NOT LOADED management state, for example. In this method, you have the option to implement any actions that you always want to execute together with the loading of the persistent attributes. For instance, you can assign values to the transient attributes of the object.

The counterpart to the IF_OS_STATE~INIT method is the IF_OS_STATE~INVALIDATE method, which the Persistence Service always calls before it discards the values of persistent attributes. This is done during the execution of the REFRESH_PERSISTENT method, when you start a new top-level transaction, when you delete a persistent object, and when you reset a transaction if the Transaction Service cancels the creation of an object in this process. In this method, you can reset the transient attributes to initial values, for example. Both in the IF_OS_STATE~INIT method and in the IF_OS_STATE~INVALIDATE method, the persistent attributes of the persistent object are filled with values, so in both methods, you can read the values of the persistent attributes of the object.

In the persistent class, you can also create your own methods or implement other interfaces, for instance, the check-agent interface, IF_OS_CHECK, without having to worry about undesired influences from automatic source code generation. You shouldn't directly edit all other generated methods of the persistent class, particularly the access methods of the attributes, because the Persistence Service overwrites them in the source code generation.

To enable you to adapt the methods of the class agent to your requirements, a concept has been implemented that is different from the approach used in the IF_OS_STATE interface of the persistent class. Instead of adapting a generated method directly in the base agent, you can redefine an inherited method in its only subclass, the class agent class. Because the generator generates the method in the class of the base agent, it doesn't overwrite your redefinition in the class agent class. But you can't change the class constructor in the class agent class, which the Persistence Service generates automatically.

5.1.5 Garbage Collection in ABAP Objects

In software technology, garbage collection refers to a mechanism that automatically releases dynamically requested memory in a running program as soon as it's no longer required by the program. In runtime environments that provide garbage collection, an application isn't required to explicitly prompt the system to release the previously used memory again. This way, the garbage collection eliminates a frequent source of error for applications that run in a runtime environment without garbage collection: If such an application repeatedly requests memory and then doesn't release it again, the memory requirement continuously increases until it eventually exceeds the memory available in the system, and the running program crashes.

The garbage collection of the ABAP runtime environment automatically removes objects from the memory at specific points in time; these objects are then no longer available from the running program via references. To test which objects the garbage collection removes, you can explicitly call it in the ABAP Debugger via the EDIT • SYSTEM FUNCTIONS • START GARBAGE COLLECTOR menu path.

The handling of persistent objects using garbage collection follows the principle that it leaves a persistent object in the memory even if the application no longer references it. The goal is to keep the Persistence Service from having to reload persistent objects that it has already loaded from the database after the garbage collection. The garbage collection therefore only removes persistent objects in the NOT LOADED management state from the memory of the running application automatically if the application doesn't reference them. For objects in the NOT LOADED management state, the removal from the memory doesn't cause any additional database access because a database access is required anyway before you can access the values of the attributes.

The behavior of the garbage collection with regard to persistent objects isn't implemented through a special handling of persistent objects in the garbage collection; instead, the Persistence Service uses the general options of object-oriented software development. Each class agent of a persistent class uses two different ways to reference managed persistent objects: usual references, also referred to as strong references, and weak references.

The class agent holds only a weak reference to a persistent object in the NOT LOADED management state, and both a strong and a weak reference to a persistent object in another management state. Because a weak reference alone doesn't prevent the garbage collection from removing the referenced object from the memory, this approach enables the garbage collection to remove a persistent object in the NOT LOADED management state from the memory, provided that the application doesn't have any further references to the persistent object.

Figure 5.3 shows an excerpt of the ABAP Debugger in which you can see the OBJECT_INFO internal table of a class agent. The class agent manages two persistent objects: the first one in the LOADED management state (PM_STATUS 2), and the second one in the NOT LOADED management state (PM_STATUS 0). The OBJECT_IREF field that contains a strong reference to the persistent object is only filled in the row with the loaded object. The class agent references the other persistent object only via a weak reference, which is stored in the OBJECT_WREF field. This object could be removed from the memory of the running application with the next run of the garbage collection.

Tables	Table Contents			
Table	/IOT/CA_SPFLI=>AGENT->OBJECT_I|			
Table Type	Sorted Table[2x16(52)]			

Line	OBJECT_ID[I(4)]	OBJECT_IREF[Reference]	OBJECT_WREF[Reference]	PM_STATUS[I(4)]
1	14	->{0:14*\CLASS=/IOT/CL_SPFLI}	->{0:15*\CLASS=CL_ABAP_WEAK_REFERENCE}	2
2	16	->{0:initial}	->{0:17*\CLASS=CL_ABAP_WEAK_REFERENCE}	0

Figure 5.3 Strong and Weak References in the Class Agent

Excursus: Weak References

In programming languages with garbage collection, references that don't prevent the garbage collection from removing the referenced object from the memory are referred to as weak references. Weak references are therefore particularly suited for implementing a management of objects with the character of a cache. As long as sufficient memory is available for the objects contained in the cache, you can access any of the objects contained via the weak reference. If the objects that are only referenced by the cache occupy too much memory, the garbage collection can release them. For the next attempt to access the released object, the cache must restore it from another source.

In ABAP, weak references are implemented via the CL_ABAP_WEAK_REFERENCE class. Listing 5.3 shows the handling of weak references. To assign a weak reference to an object, you generate an object of the CL_ABAP_WEAK_REFERENCE class and transfer a strong reference to the object to be referenced. You can use the GET method to request a strong reference for a weak reference. If the garbage collection has removed the object with the weak reference from the memory in the meantime, the GET method returns a NULL reference.

```
DATA: rf_spfli          TYPE REF TO /iot/cl_spfli,
      rf_weak_ref_spfli TYPE REF TO cl_abap_weak_reference.

* Generate a weak reference for a strong reference
CREATE OBJECT rf_weak_ref_spfli
  EXPORTING
    oref = rf_spfli.

* Request a strong reference for the weak reference
rf_spfli ?= rf_weak_ref_spfli->get( ).
```

Listing 5.3 Handling Weak References

5.2   Transaction Service

The following sections detail which information is stored by the Transaction Manager and every single transaction in its attributes. You also learn how the Transaction Service can reset persistent objects in the memory to a state in which they previously were — without accessing the database.

5.2.1   Implementation of the Transaction Manager and the Transactions

The IF_OS_TRANSACTION_MANAGER and IF_OS_TRANSACTION interfaces, via which you can access the Transaction Manager and the transactions from your applications, are implemented in the CL_OS_TRANSACTION_MANAGER and CL_OS_TRANSACTION classes.

Figure 5.4 shows which associations exist between the Transaction Manager and the running transactions for a sample scenario with a top-level transaction and two running subtransactions. When you start or end a transaction, the transaction informs the Transaction Manager about the start of the transaction that is now the current transaction. The Transaction Manager can use this information to update its two attributes, TOP_TRANSACTION and CURRENT_TRANSACTION, by which the Transaction Manager respectively references the top-level transaction and the current transaction.

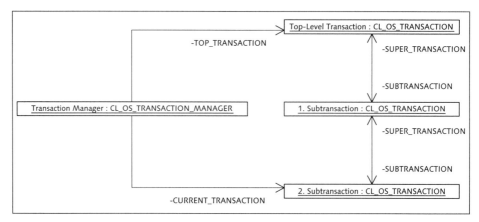

Figure 5.4 Object Diagram with Components of the Transaction Service

Each transaction respectively holds one reference to the superordinate transaction (SUPER_TRANSACTION) and to the subordinate transaction (SUBTRANSACTION). If a transaction contains a NULL reference in the SUPER_TRANSACTION attribute, it's a top-level transaction. The SUBTRANSACTION attribute contains a NULL reference if it's the subtransaction at the lowest level.

Besides the references to other transactions, each transaction contains the following additional attributes:

▶ CHAINED
The CHAINED attribute indicates whether you've started the transaction through a concatenation with a previous transaction. It has the abap_true value if you've created the transaction via the END_AND_CHAIN method or the UNDO_AND_CHAIN method of another transaction; it has the abap_false value if you've created the transaction via the Transaction Manager.

▶ CHECK_AGENTS
The CHECK_AGENTS attribute contains an internal table with references to all check agents that you've registered in the transaction. If you end a transaction, it successively calls the method for the consistency check in every registered check agent based on this table.

▶ DATA_SAVE_STATE
The saving status in top-level transactions inform you about whether the implemented changes to persistent objects have been written to the database. Possible values include the following:

▶ `OSCON_SSTATUS_INITIAL` (0): Object Services haven't yet started to write the changes from the transaction to the database.

▶ `OSCON_SSTATUS_SAVING` (1): Object Services currently write the changes from the transaction to the database. The transaction sets the status before it starts writing the changes to persistent objects to the database. It remains set until the transaction has executed the `COMMIT WORK` statement in the object-oriented transaction mode or until the system informs the transaction in the compatibility mode that the execution of the `COMMIT WORK` statement is completed.

▶ `OSCON_SSTATUS_SUCCESS` (2): Object Services successfully wrote the changes made in the transaction to the database.

▶ `OSCON_SSTATUS_FAILED` (3): Errors occurred when the changes to persistent objects were saved or when the update modules were executed synchronously.

▶ `TRANSACTION_STATE`
In the `TRANSACTION_STATE` attribute, the transaction manages its current transaction status (*see* Section 3.3.9, Transaction Statuses, in Chapter 3).

▶ `UNDO_RELEVANT`
The `UNDO_RELEVANT` attribute indicates whether the undo mechanism is activated (*see* Section 3.3.8, Undo Mechanism for Persistent Objects, in Chapter 3).

▶ `UPDATE_MODE`
The `UPDATE_MODE` attribute stores the selected update mode (*see* Section 3.3.6, Updated Modes, in Chapter 3).

▶ `FLAG_UPDT_MODE_CHANGED`
The `FLAG_UPDT_MODE_CHANGED` attribute specifies for a top-level transaction in the compatibility mode whether you have already changed the update mode for this transaction. You may change the update mode in the compatibility mode in a running top-level transaction only once. In the object-oriented transaction mode, this differentiation isn't required because you must not change the update mode of a top-level transaction after you've started the transaction.

5.2.2 Undo Management

When you reset a transaction, the Transaction Service enables you to also reset the persistent objects in the memory to the state which they had before the transaction started. For this purpose, Object Services generate a copy of the original values of all persistent attributes of a persistent object when you implement the first change to this persistent object in the running transaction. If you reset the transaction with one of the UNDO methods at a later point in time, Object Services restore the original state based on the previously created copy.

The class agents of the persistent classes manage the information about which changes you've made to the persistent objects. If you work with any persistent attribute, the persistent object triggers different events, for example, if you change the value of a persistent attribute or create a new persistent object. The corresponding class agent is registered as an event handler for all persistent objects of the corresponding persistent class. Every persistent object uses the event mechanism to inform the class agent about actions that the Transaction Service will possibly undo later on. Within the handling of the events that have occurred, the class agent remembers the management state that the persistent object had when the transaction was started. Also, it stores a copy of the original values of all persistent attributes if required. This way, the class agent enables you to undo changes to persistent objects in the memory using the UNDO methods of a transaction.

To create a copy of the persistent attributes of a persistent object and to restore the original state at a later point in time if required, the class agent uses the GET and SET methods from the IF_OS_STATE interface, which Object Services automatically generate for each persistent class. The structure of these methods is based on the memento design pattern. The memento design pattern enables you to freeze the current state of an object by creating a copy of all attributes of the object in an additional object. By means of the memento object, you can restore the frozen state of the object at a later point in time. A call of the IF_OS_STATE~GET method on a persistent object generates a status object of the CL_OS_STATE class, which doesn't implement the IF_OS_STATE interface despite the similar name. This status object temporarily stores all information that is required to reset the persistent object with its attributes to the original state if required. Using the IF_OS_STATE~SET method, the caller can reset a persistent object to a previous state by transferring a previously generated status object to the method.

The class agent calls the IF_OS_STATE~GET method of a persistent object when you use an access method in the running transaction to access the value of an attribute of the persistent object for the first time in write mode. Because the call is made before the access method changes the value of the attribute, the created status object still represents the original state of the persistent object. If you reset a transaction, the Transaction Service calls the IF_OS_STATE~SET method on all changed persistent objects and transfers a corresponding status object that it created before you made the changes.

The IF_OS_STATE~GET and IF_OS_STATE~SET methods call the SET_STATE_FROM_OBJECT or SET_OBJECT_FROM_STATE method on the status object of the CL_OS_STATE class to copy and restore the state of the persistent object. These in turn use the SYSTEM-CALL statement to call system functions in the ABAP kernel that copy the values of the persistent attribute from the object or to the object. Due to the use of the system functions, you can't view the implementation details of these methods in the ABAP source code. SAP also recommends using the system functions only in an automated mode via Object Services. You shouldn't call the system functions directly in your applications.

Figure 5.5 summarizes the previously described call hierarchy in the undo management. The figure shows an example of how Object Services call the system function with which they create a copy of the original state of a persistent object when you call an access method for changing the destination in a flight plan.

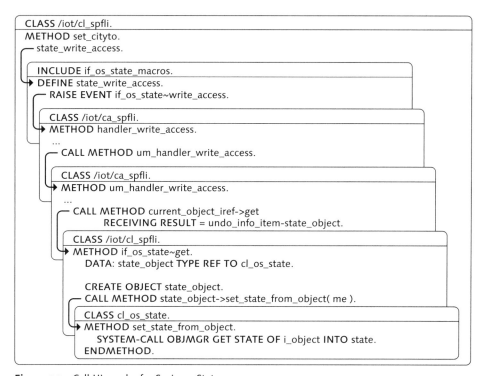

```
CLASS /iot/cl_spfli.
  METHOD set_cityto.
    state_write_access.

    INCLUDE if_os_state_macros.
    DEFINE state_write_access.
      RAISE EVENT if_os_state~write_access.

      CLASS /iot/ca_spfli.
        METHOD handler_write_access.
        ...
          CALL METHOD um_handler_write_access.

          CLASS /iot/ca_spfli.
            METHOD um_handler_write_access.
            ...
              CALL METHOD current_object_iref->get
                   RECEIVING RESULT = undo_info_item-state_object.
              CLASS /iot/cl_spfli.
                METHOD if_os_state~get.
                  DATA: state_object TYPE REF TO cl_os_state.

                  CREATE OBJECT state_object.
                  CALL METHOD state_object->set_state_from_object( me ).
                  CLASS cl_os_state.
                    METHOD set_state_from_object.
                      SYSTEM-CALL OBJMGR GET STATE OF i_object INTO state.
                    ENDMETHOD.
```

Figure 5.5 Call Hierarchy for Saving a State

Every automatically generated access method in a persistent class starts with the call of a macro. For a write access to an attribute, it's the STATE_WRITE_ACCESS macro. The macro triggers the WRITE_ACCESS event that is defined in the IF_OS_STATE interface. The HANDLER_WRITE_ACCESS method of the respective class agent is defined as the event handler for this event. Within the event handling by the class agent, the class agent calls the IF_OS_STATE~GET method of the persistent object from the UM_HANDLER_WRITE_ACCESS method. The IF_OS_STATE~GET method of the persistent object creates a status object and then uses the status object's SET_STATE_FROM_OBJECT method to create a copy of its own attributes. For this purpose, the status object uses a system function that it calls via the SYSTEM-CALL statement. Only when the event handling is completed, does the originally called access method change the value of the persistent attribute.

5.3 CL_OS_SYSTEM

Besides the methods for determining a reference to the Transaction Manager, the Query Manager, the Instance Manager, and the Persistency Manager, as well as the methods for setting the transaction mode and the update mode, the CL_OS_SYSTEM class also includes further static methods. For example, you can use the GET_CLASS_AGENT method to request a reference to the class agent of a persistent class. You must transfer the name of the persistent class as a parameter. Because you don't access a static attribute of the class agent directly when you use this method, the instantiation of the class agent isn't executed before the execution of the processing block but during the execution of the GET_CLASS_AGENT method.

Consequently, the GET_CLASS_AGENT method can be an alternative for handling the sequence problem when you set a transaction mode, which was discussed in Section 3.3.5, Transaction Modes, in Chapter 3. Instead of having to set the transaction mode in a separate processing block and being able to work with class agents in another processing block only then, you can first set the transaction mode in a processing block and then request references to the class agents using the GET_CLASS_AGENT method.

Listing 5.4 shows how you can set the transaction mode within a processing block using the GET_CLASS_AGENT method and instantiate a persistent object. Because the class agent isn't instantiated until the processing of the GET_CLASS_AGENT method, the transaction mode isn't yet set when you call INIT_AND_SET_MODES.

```
DATA: rf_ca_spfli   TYPE REF TO /iot/ca_spfli,
      rf_spfli      TYPE REF TO /iot/cl_spfli,
      st_class_key  TYPE seoclskey.

* Set transaction mode:
* Application runs in object-oriented transaction mode
cl_os_system=>init_and_set_modes(
  i_external_commit = abap_false ).

* Request reference to the class agent
st_class_key-clsname = '/IOT/CL_SPFLI'.
rf_ca_spfli ?= cl_os_system=>get_class_agent( st_class_key ).

* Instantiate flight plan
rf_spfli =
  rf_ca_spfli->get_persistent(
    i_carrid = 'AA'
    i_connid = '17' ).
```

Listing 5.4 Using the GET_CLASS_AGENT Method

You can use the GET_CLASS_AGENT_INFO method to request information on a class agent and the persistent class that is managed by this class agent. The returned structure of the OSTYP_CA_INFO type contains, for example, the class name and the class GUID of the class agent as well as the class name and the class GUID of the managed persistent class.

The two methods described are also helpful if you write generic ABAP source code, that is, methods that are supposed to work with objects from any persistent class, for example.

Moreover, the CL_OS_SYSTEM class contains multiple static attributes whose value you can also read outside the class:

▶ ACTIVE_CLASS_AGENT
The ACTIVE_CLASS_AGENT internal table contains references to all class agents that you've already used in the running internal session. This table can form the basis if you want to consecutively implement a certain action with every class agent used. You can also use this table to check whether you've already worked with objects of a specific persistent class in the running program.

▶ EXTERNAL_COMMIT

Using the EXTERNAL_COMMIT static attribute, you can determine in which transaction mode your application runs. Similar to the I_EXTERNAL_COMMIT parameter for setting the transaction mode, abap_false stands for the object-oriented transaction mode, and abap_true stands for the compatibility mode.

▶ INIT_STATE

The system state in the INIT_STATE attribute specifies whether Object Services and the transaction and update mode have already been initialized in the current internal session. If the attribute is still set to its initial value 0, this hasn't been done yet. During the initialization, the attribute adopts the value 1 and then value 2 at the end of the initialization.

5.4   Summary

This chapter described how the functions of Object Services, which were described in Chapters 2 through 4, are implemented. This knowledge makes it easier to create your own enhancements of Object Services and to understand the enhancement of Object Services that are described in the following chapters. Also, this knowledge is helpful if you search for errors in applications that are used by Object Services.

Based on this knowledge, the following chapters will introduce enhancements to Object Services that have proven to be useful in many real-life projects.

If you can't find a function you need in Object Services, you can add it yourself. This chapter presents some enhancements that are used in real-world scenarios.

6 Useful Enhancements for Practical Use

This chapter describes how you can enhance Object Services with additional functions that are often required in practical use. This includes methods with which you can ensure that the Persistence Service reloads all persistent objects from the database with the next access or removes them completely from the management. Then you learn about different methods with which you can transfer data from the attributes of an object to a structure or from a structure to the attributes of an object. These methods help you display the data from an object in the user interface and write the user's input to the object.

6.1 Reloading Objects from the Database

If you request your class agent to instantiate an object that you've already instantiated before, the Persistence Service ensures that you receive a reference to the already-instantiated object. Because this action doesn't require access to the database, the Persistence Service thus reduces the load of the database system. In specific situations, it makes sense to bypass this mechanism intentionally to load the current status of a persistent object from the database.

Situations in which it makes sense to reload the persistent objects from the database include the reexecution of a selection by the user. The user expects to view the current data after the selection. Also, if you want to provide the users with an option to refresh the presented data explicitly, you must reload the persistent objects from the database.

Section 3.4.2, State Transitions for Persistent Objects That Already Exist in the Database, in Chapter 3, already discussed how to reload individual objects from the database in a targeted manner. Before a new selection or before the refresh of all data presented, however, you have to reload not only individual persistent objects but also all persistent objects of a class or even all persistent objects that are loaded in the running program, independent of the class, to be able to display current data.

The following sections present two universal methods that you can use to reload all loaded objects of a class or all persistent objects independent of the class from the database. Both methods transfer the persistent objects from the LOADED management state to the NOT LOADED management state. The methods don't affect the persistent objects in other management states.

You can't simply reload newly created, changed, or deleted objects from the database because the database doesn't yet contain the current state of the objects. The IF_OS_FACTORY~REFRESH_PERSISTENT method of the class agent isn't designed to undo changes to persistent objects. The method therefore throws an exception if you call it with a persistent object in the NEW, CHANGED, or DELETED management state. If you want to reload persistent objects from these management states from the database, you must first undo the changes using the Transaction Service. Then you can call one of the two methods presented.

Listing 6.1 includes a method that you can call if you want to reload all persistent objects of a class from the database. For this purpose, you need to provide the method with a reference to the class agent of the persistent class whose persistent objects you want to reload. The method sets the objects to the NOT LOADED management state only. The Persistence Service then reloads the object from the database when you call a method for instantiation or call an access method of a persistent object's attribute.

```
METHOD refresh_objects_by_agent.
  DATA: ri_object     TYPE REF TO if_os_state,
        ro_object     TYPE REF TO object,
        ta_ro_objects TYPE ostyp_ref_tab.

* Determine all objects in the LOADED management state
  ta_ro_objects =
    im_rf_agent->if_os_ca_instance~get_loaded( ).

  LOOP AT ta_ro_objects INTO ro_object.
*   Typecast: OBJECT => IF_OS_STATE
    TRY.
        ri_object ?= ro_object.
```

```
      CATCH cx_sy_move_cast_error.
        CONTINUE.
      ENDTRY.

*    Execute refresh for currently processed object
      TRY.
          im_rf_agent->if_os_factory~refresh_persistent(
            ri_object ).
        CATCH cx_os_object_not_refreshable.
          CONTINUE.
      ENDTRY.
    ENDLOOP.
ENDMETHOD.
```

Listing 6.1 Method for Refreshing All Persistent Objects of a Class

The REFRESH_OBJECTS_BY_AGENT method uses the transferred class agent to determine all persistent objects of a persistent class in the LOADED management state. With each of these objects, you then individually call the IF_OS_FACTORY~REFRESH_PERSISTENT method of the class agent that transfers the respective persistent object to the NOT LOADED management state.

In the inheritance structures between the persistent classes, the REFRESH_OBJECTS_BY_AGENT method processes only objects that belong directly to the persistent class that the transferred class agent manages. Persistent objects that only belong to superclasses or also to subclasses aren't transferred to the NOT LOADED management state.

The REFRESH_ALL_OBJECTS method presented in Listing 6.2 sets all persistent objects from the LOADED management state to the NOT LOADED management state irrespective of the class to which the persistent objects belong. You don't need to transfer any parameters to this method when it's called.

```
METHOD refresh_all_objects.
  DATA: rf_agent              TYPE REF TO cl_os_ca_common,
        wa_active_class_agent TYPE ostyp_ca_info.

* Call REFRESH method for every active class agent for all
* managed objects in management state LOADED
  LOOP AT cl_os_system=>active_class_agent
        INTO wa_active_class_agent.
*    Typecast: OBJECT -> CL_OS_CA_COMMON
```

```
    TRY.
        rf_agent ?= wa_active_class_agent-class_agent_ref.
      CATCH cx_sy_move_cast_error.
*       (Unexpected) Error in Typecast
*       => Do not execute REFRESH for this agent
        CONTINUE.
    ENDTRY.


*   Call REFRESH for every unchanged persistent object managed
*   by the agent
    /iot/cl_agent_services=>refresh_objects_by_agent(
      rf_agent ).
  ENDLOOP.

ENDMETHOD.
```

Listing 6.2 Method for Refreshing All Persistent Objects of All Classes

The REFRESH_ALL_OBJECTS method uses the static attribute, ACTIVE_CLASS_AGENT, of the CL_OS_SYSTEM class to determine all class agents that you've used in the running program so far. With each class agent, the method then calls the previously presented method, REFRESH_OBJECTS_BY_AGENT, once. This method in turn calls the IF_OS_FACTORY~REFRESH_PERSISTENT method of the respective class agent for all persistent objects in the LOADED management state that are managed by the respective class agent.

6.2   Release of Objects No Longer Required

For persistent objects that you not only want to reload from the database, but also completely remove from the management of the class agent, you can use the IF_OS_FACTORY~RELEASE method of the class agent for individual objects. Similar to the refresh, it's often required to release not only individual objects but also many objects.

From the perspective of memory consumption, it isn't absolutely necessary to remove objects completely from the management. The garbage collection automatically removes persistent objects from the memory that aren't in the NOT LOADED management state and that are only referenced by the class agent.

You can release objects of persistent classes in the management states, NOT LOADED, LOADED, and TRANSIENT. To release all objects of a class or all objects of all persistent classes, you can use methods that are similar to those presented earlier in Section 6.1, Reloading Objects from the Database. Instead of only requesting the objects in the LOADED management state from the class agent, you can also determine all objects in the NOT LOADED and TRANSIENT management states in the same way. With every object determined this way, you then call the class agent's IF_OS_FACTORY~RELEASE method instead of the IF_OS_FACTORY~REFRESH_PERSISTENT method.

6.3   Conversion Between Object and Structure

Not all services that are provided by SAP NetWeaver AS ABAP are designed to directly work with objects in an object-oriented way. Numerous services that still facilitate the development of applications today have been created when object-oriented components were not yet supported in the ABAP language.

To use such services in an application that works with persistent objects, you need to convert the data from the persistent objects into a suitable format. Usually, this involves structured internal tables. Here it's possible to manually read the value of every single attribute of every persistent object and transfer it to a structure. However, the development of this procedure is very tedious, and the resulting ABAP source code is hard to read and thus difficult to maintain. Whenever you remove an attribute of the persistent class, add a new one, or rename an existing one, you would have to manually adapt all locations at which you implemented a manual conversion between object and structure.

This section therefore presents two simple methods to implement this conversion automatically. They transfer all values of a persistent object's attributes to the correspondent components of a structure or, vice versa, from the components of a structure to the attributes of a persistent object, respectively. They are similar to the MOVE-CORRESPONDING statement of classic ABAP, which transfers the values of a structure's components to the correspondent components of another structure. The methods are formulated universally so that you can use them for any persistent classes with any attributes. If you use methods of this type, you don't need to adapt all locations in the ABAP source code in which you implement the conversion between objects and structures when you enhance or change the attributes of a persistent class later.

6.3.1 Reading Attribute Values from a Persistent Object

To read values from the attributes of a persistent object and transfer them to a structure, you can use the OBJECT_TO_STRUCTURE method presented in Listing 6.3. For this purpose, use the IM_RO_INPUT parameter to pass a reference to the method that references the persistent object from which you want to transfer the values of the attributes to the structure. Via the EX_ST_OUTPUT parameter, the method returns a structure in which all components are filled for which a correspondent attribute exists in the transferred object.

```
METHOD object_to_structure.
  DATA: rf_structdescr TYPE REF TO cl_abap_structdescr,
        v_method_name   TYPE seomtdname,
        wa_component    TYPE abap_compdescr.

  FIELD-SYMBOLS: <v_component> TYPE ANY.

* Request description of transferred structure
  rf_structdescr ?=
    cl_abap_typedescr=>describe_by_data( ex_st_output ).

* Loop via all components of the transferred structure
  LOOP AT rf_structdescr->components INTO wa_component.
*    Set the field symbol to the component of the transferred
*    structure
    ASSIGN COMPONENT wa_component-name
           OF STRUCTURE ex_st_output
           TO <v_component>.

*    Compose the name of the GET method
    CONCATENATE 'GET_' wa_component-name INTO v_method_name.

*    Determine the value of the attribute via a dynamic call of
*    the GET method and write the value to the structure
    TRY.
        CALL METHOD im_ro_input->(v_method_name)
          RECEIVING
            result = <v_component>.
```

```
      CATCH cx_sy_dyn_call_illegal_method.
        CONTINUE.
      ENDTRY.
    ENDLOOP.
ENDMETHOD.
```

Listing 6.3 Method That Transfers the Values of the Persistent Object's Attributes to a Structure

The `OBJECT_TO_STRUCTURE` method works with a type object that describes the structure to which the method transfers the values from the attributes of the object. The method uses a `LOOP` loop to successively transfer the value of an attribute to a component of the structure. For this purpose, the currently processed component is assigned to the `<v_component>` field symbol. The method uses the `GET_` prefix and the name of the component to compose the name of the access method of the corresponding attribute of the persistent object.

Using a dynamic method call, the `OBJECT_TO_STRUCTURE` method tries to call the access method for an attribute that has the same name as a component of the structure. If the call is successful, the correspondingly assigned field symbol directly writes the value to the component of the structure. If no method with the composed name exists in the object, or if the method doesn't have the Public visibility, an exception of the `CX_SY_DYN_CALL_ILLEGAL_METHOD` class is raised. In this case, the original value of the processed component of the structure is kept, and the method continues with the processing of the next component.

Excursus: Run Time Type Services and Type Objects

The Run Time Type Services (RTTS) in ABAP comprise the Run Time Type Identification (RTTI) and the Run Time Type Creation (RTTC). RTTI enables you to obtain detailed information on a data type in a running program. For example, you can determine to which class a referenced object belongs, whether it implements a specific interface, or which components belong to a structure. The system provides this information via objects of *type classes*, the *type objects*. The names of the type classes start with `CL_ABAP_` and end with `DESCR` (descriptor).

The type objects are also used within RTTC. The goal of RTTC isn't to describe the type of existing variables or objects but to dynamically create data objects at runtime, whereas these data objects have a type that you haven't yet defined during development. Here, you use the type objects to initially define the desired type in detail and to reserve the memory for a data object of this type.

Similar to the MOVE-CORRESPONDING statement, the OBJECT_TO_STRUCTURE method transfers the values of the attributes for which a component with an identical name exists in the structure. However, it doesn't provide the calling program with any information whether it read all attributes of the persistent class or whether it was able to fill all components of the structure with values. With the type objects for the returned structure or for the transferred object, you have all of the information at hand that is required to enhance the method with such functions if required.

Besides the intended use of the method with persistent objects, it's also suited for automatic reading of attribute values from usual objects. The only prerequisite is that methods exist whose names start with the GET_ prefix and only have a returning parameter called RESULT.

6.3.2 Writing Attribute Values to a Persistent Object

You can also dynamically implement a method for the other way around; that is, transfer values from the components of a structure to the attributes of a persistent object. Listing 6.4 shows the STRUCTURE_TO_OBJECT method. You can use the IM_ST_INPUT parameter to pass a structure, from whose components you want to transfer the values to the attributes of a persistent object, to this method. You transfer the persistent object to the method via the IM_RO_OUTPUT parameter.

```
METHOD structure_to_object.
   DATA: rf_structdescr TYPE REF TO cl_abap_structdescr,
         ta_parameters  TYPE abap_parmbind_tab,
         v_method_name  TYPE seomtdname,
         wa_component   TYPE abap_compdescr,
         wa_parameter   TYPE abap_parmbind.

   FIELD-SYMBOLS: <v_component> TYPE ANY.

*  Request a description of the transferred structure
   rf_structdescr ?=
     cl_abap_typedescr=>describe_by_data( im_st_input ).

*  Loop via all components of the transferred structure
   LOOP AT rf_structdescr->components INTO wa_component.
*    Set the field symbol to the component of the transferred
*    structure
```

```
ASSIGN COMPONENT wa_component-name
       OF STRUCTURE im_st_input
       TO <v_component>.

*   Compose the name of the SET method
    CONCATENATE 'SET_' wa_component-name INTO v_method_name.

*   Prepare the parameter table for the dynamic call:
*   - You will be transferring an exporting parameter
*   - Name of the parameter: "I_<attribute name>"
*   - Value to be transferred: Value in the component of the
*     structure
    CLEAR ta_parameters.
    wa_parameter-kind = cl_abap_objectdescr=>exporting.
    CONCATENATE 'I_' wa_component-name INTO wa_parameter-name.
    GET REFERENCE OF <v_component> INTO wa_parameter-value.
    INSERT wa_parameter INTO TABLE ta_parameters.

*   Change the value of the attribute via a dynamic call of
*   the SET method
    TRY.
        CALL METHOD im_ro_output->(v_method_name)
          PARAMETER-TABLE
            ta_parameters.
      CATCH cx_sy_dyn_call_illegal_method.
        CONTINUE.
    ENDTRY.

  ENDLOOP.
ENDMETHOD.
```

Listing 6.4 Method That Transfers the Values from a Structure to the Attributes of a Persistent Object

This method also works with a type object that it creates for the transferred structure. In the loop via the components of the structure, the method respectively assigns one component of the structure to a field symbol. Then the method composes a possible name of an access method of an attribute of the persistent object using the SET_ prefix and the name of the component.

The name of the importing parameter of a SET method differs from method to method because it respectively contains the name of the attribute that you can change using the method. Prior to the dynamic call of the SET method, the STRUC-TURE_TO_OBJECT method must therefore prepare an internal table that includes the parameters. It transfers the value of the corresponding component of the structure to the access method of the attribute.

If no SET method for a component exists in the transferred object, the dynamic method call fails. If a corresponding attribute exists, but you may access it in read mode only from the outside, the method also doesn't assign a new value to this attribute and continues processing the next component of the structure. Because no SET method exists for the attributes that form the business key of a class — just like for the value attributes that you've explicitly assigned with the Read Only changeability in the persistence representation — the STRUCTURE_TO_OBJECT method doesn't change the values of these attributes in any case.

6.3.3 Structures in Connection with Persistent Classes

You can use the two previously presented methods both with structures that contain a corresponding component for each attribute of a persistent class and with structures that contain corresponding components only for a subset of the attributes. The following sections present various options to define structures of both types statically and dynamically.

**Structures That Contain a Corresponding Component
for Each Attribute of a Persistent Class**

You have various options to generate a structure with all attributes of a persistent class for your application that you can use with the two methods presented. The database table, which you've assigned to the persistent class in the persistence representation, contains at least one corresponding field for each persistent attribute. When you create a structured variable with the database table as the type, you must take into account the following differences:

▸ If you used different names for the persistent attributes in the persistence representation than for the fields in the database table, then the names of the components of a structure that you've defined via the database table differ from the names of the persistent attributes. As a result, the previously presented methods can't automatically transfer the values for these attributes.

▸ The database tables contain no fields that correspond to the transient attributes of the persistent class.

▸ If you've assigned multiple database tables to the persistent class in the persistence representation, you possibly need to work with various variables or create a view in the data dictionary that includes the fields of all database tables assigned.

▸ If you work with persistent references, the database table contains two fields of the OS_GUID type but no fields with a reference type.

▸ The database table also respectively contains a field of the OS_GUID type for the instance GUIDs and the type identifier. The persistent class, however, contains neither attributes nor corresponding access methods for these fields.

▸ The database table's key usually contains a field with the client to which the respective data record belongs. The Persistence Service doesn't provide this field in the persistence representation for assignment, so the persistent class normally doesn't include an attribute with the client.

As an alternative to a variable with a database table as the type, you can also create your own structure that contains a component of the same name and the same type for each attribute of the persistent class. In this case, you can either create a structure in the data dictionary or define the structure in the ABAP source code using the TYPES statement.

Via the Run Time Type Creation (RTTC), as of Release 6.40, it's also possible in SAP NetWeaver AS ABAP to dynamically create a suitable type at runtime. Instead of manually defining a suitable structure at development time, you can automatically create a structure in the running program that contains a corresponding component for each persistent attribute of a persistent object. Because the structure is always created in compliance with the current definition of the persistent class in this procedure, you don't need to implement any manual adaptations to the structure definitions if you change the definition of the attributes in the persistent class later.

Listing 6.5 contains a method that uses RTTC to create a structure that contains a component of the same name and the same type for each attribute of the persistent object passed to the method via its IM_RO_INPUT parameter.

```
METHOD create_structure.
  DATA: rf_classdescr       TYPE REF TO cl_abap_classdescr,
        rf_structure_type   TYPE REF TO cl_abap_structdescr,
        st_component        TYPE abap_componentdescr,
```

```
      ta_components       TYPE abap_component_tab,
      wa_attribute        TYPE abap_attrdescr.

* Request description of the transferred object
  rf_classdescr ?=
    cl_abap_typedescr=>describe_by_object_ref( im_ro_input ).

* Prepare internal table with components of the structure:
* Create a component with the same name and the same type
* for each attribute
  LOOP AT rf_classdescr->attributes INTO wa_attribute.
    st_component-name = wa_attribute-name.
    st_component-type =
      rf_classdescr->get_attribute_type( wa_attribute-name ).
    APPEND st_component TO ta_components.
  ENDLOOP.

* Create a type object for the structure to be newly created
  rf_structure_type =
    cl_abap_structdescr=>create( ta_components ).

* Create a data object with the new structure
  CREATE DATA re_dr_structure TYPE HANDLE rf_structure_type.
ENDMETHOD.
```

Listing 6.5 Method That Dynamically Creates a Structure for the Attributes of an Object

The CREATE_STRUCTURE method works with a type object that describes the transferred persistent object. In a LOOP loop, the method uses information from the type object to fill the ta_components internal table, which then contains all components of the structure to be created. With this internal table, the method then creates a type object to define the new structure. The CREATE DATA statement uses this type object to generate a data object in the memory of the running program that uses the structure that was created dynamically as the type.

The method returns a data reference to the created structure as a return value. For example, the calling program of the method can assign this data reference to a field symbol to work with the individual components of the structure or to call one of the methods of Listing 6.3 or Listing 6.4 (shown earlier) with the entire structure as the parameter.

Business Key Structure for a Persistent Class

Besides a structure, which contains a field for each attribute of a persistent class, you often need a structure that includes the fields of the business key of a persistent class in Object Services. For example, both the IF_OS_CA_PERSISTENCY~GET_ PERSISTENT_BY_KEY method, with which you can instantiate persistent objects (see Section 2.2, Instantiating Persistent Objects, in Chapter 2), and the IF_OS_ FACTORY~CREATE_PERSISTENT_BY_KE method, with which you can create persistent object (see Section 3.1.2, IF_OS_FACTORY~CREATE_PERSISTENT_BY_KEY, in Chapter 3), expect the business key in the form of a structure as the parameter.

The three presented options are also available for creating a business key structure: You can define a structure type in the data dictionary or via the TYPES statement or dynamically generate the structure via RTTC .. There is an additional option for the business key

A structure type with the components of the business key already exists in the class agents of persistent classes, whose persistence representation includes a definition of a business key. This type is defined with the name TYP_BUSINESS_KEY in the protected section of the class of the base agent and includes the components in the sequence in which the class agent's methods expect them. Due to the Protected visibility, you can use this type directly only in the class agent.

To access the type also outside the class agent, you can create another type that is defined referring to the already-existing. If you assign the Public visibility to this type you define, you can work with this type also in other classes or in reports, for example. Because in this kind of definition you refer to the type that the Persistence Service automatically adapts to all changes in the persistence representation, you need to define the type for each persistent class only once and can then work with it without having to manually adjust it to possible changes to the components of the business key.

Figure 6.1 shows an example for the definition of a type with the structure of a business key, which you can also use outside the class agent. A type with the name, TYP_BUSINESS_KEY_PUBLIC, is defined in the class agent of the persistent class with the flights from the flight data model. Instead of defining the individual components, the type is defined by referring to the already-existing type, TYP_ BUSINESS_KEY. Due to the Public visibility, you can directly address the type via the /iot/ca_sflight=>typ_business_key_public expression also outside the class, for example, to create variables of this type.

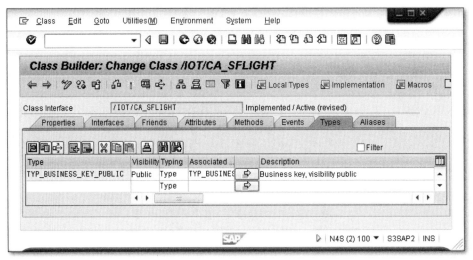

Figure 6.1 Publicly Available Business Key Structure in the Class Agent

6.4 Use of Persistent Objects in User Interfaces

The various technologies with which you can create graphical user interfaces in ABAP are designed for working with structured data and not for direct handling of objects. More recent technologies, such as the SAP Control Framework or Web Dynpro ABAP, are already implemented using object-oriented language elements; each UI element, for instance, a table or a tree, is an object. However, if you want to present data in these UI elements, it isn't possible, to transfer a persistent object to a UI element directly. The various UI elements expect that you transfer the data to be presented in the form of a value with an elementary type, in the form of a structure, or in the form of a structured internal table.

The previously presented methods for converting data from objects into structures or vice versa facilitate the necessary transition from object orientation to the structured world.

6.4.1 SAP Control Framework

In ABAP, the SAP Control Framework enables you to compose user interfaces, which are displayed in the SAP GUI, from various UI elements. These elements are referred to as controls. The UI elements that you can address via the SAP Control Framework include those for presenting data in the form of lists (ALV grid control) and trees (tree control) but also those for presenting websites, images, or calendars.

To present data in the form of a list in an ALV grid control, you must transfer a structured internal table to the control. Each line of the internal table corresponds to a line in the list output, and each component of the structure corresponds to a possible column in the list output.

Listing 6.6 shows how to display the data from persistent objects in an ALV grid control. In the presentation in the user interface, a line of the list corresponds to an object and a column of the list to an attribute of the persistent class.

```
DATA: rf_ca_sflight     TYPE REF TO /iot/ca_sflight,
      ri_query_manager  TYPE REF TO if_os_query_manager,
      ri_query          TYPE REF TO if_os_query,
      ro_sflight        TYPE REF TO object,
      st_sflight        TYPE sflight,
      ta_ro_sflight     TYPE osreftab,
      ta_st_sflight     TYPE STANDARD TABLE OF sflight.


rf_ca_sflight = /iot/ca_sflight=>agent.

* Instantiate all flights of Lufthansa carrier via a
* query with the Query Service
ri_query_manager = cl_os_system=>get_query_manager( ).
ri_query =
  ri_query_manager->create_query(
    i_filter = 'CARRID = ''LH''').

ta_ro_sflight =
  rf_ca_sflight->if_os_ca_persistency~get_persistent_by_query(
    ri_query ).

* Convert the table with references to persistent objects into
* a structured table
LOOP AT ta_ro_sflight INTO ro_sflight.
  CALL METHOD /iot/cl_obj_struct_converter=>object_to_structure
    EXPORTING
      im_ro_input  = ro_sflight
    IMPORTING
      ex_st_output = st_sflight.
```

```
  APPEND st_sflight TO ta_st_sflight.
ENDLOOP.

* Display the data from the structured table in an ALV grid
* control
CALL FUNCTION 'REUSE_ALV_GRID_DISPLAY'
  EXPORTING
    i_structure_name = 'SFLIGHT'
  TABLES
    t_outtab         = ta_st_sflight.
```

Listing 6.6 Presentation of Data from Persistent Objects in an ALV Grid Control

Listing 6.6 initially instantiates all flights of the Lufthansa airline carrier from the flight data model with a query via the Query Service. Each instantiated flight is then transferred individually to the OBJECT_TO_STRUCTURE method, which has been presented in Section 6.3.1, Reading Attribute Values from a Persistent Object. The method transfers the data from the attributes of the persistent object to a structure. The structures generated this way are collected in the TA_ST_SFLIGHT internal table.

This internal table is then transferred to the REUSE_ALV_GRID_DISPLAY function module for presenting the data in the ALV grid control. This function module displays the transferred data in the user interface (see Figure 6.2).

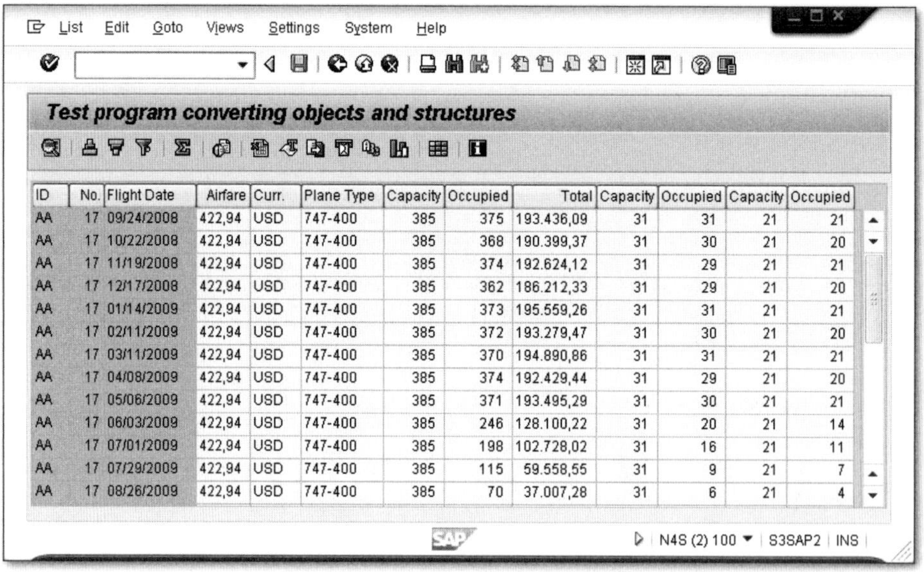

ID	No.	Flight Date	Airfare	Curr.	Plane Type	Capacity	Occupied	Total	Capacity	Occupied	Capacity	Occupied
AA	17	09/24/2008	422,94	USD	747-400	385	375	193.436,09	31	31	21	21
AA	17	10/22/2008	422,94	USD	747-400	385	368	190.399,37	31	30	21	20
AA	17	11/19/2008	422,94	USD	747-400	385	374	192.624,12	31	29	21	21
AA	17	12/17/2008	422,94	USD	747-400	385	362	186.212,33	31	29	21	20
AA	17	01/14/2009	422,94	USD	747-400	385	373	195.559,26	31	31	21	21
AA	17	02/11/2009	422,94	USD	747-400	385	372	193.279,47	31	30	21	20
AA	17	03/11/2009	422,94	USD	747-400	385	370	194.890,86	31	31	21	21
AA	17	04/08/2009	422,94	USD	747-400	385	374	192.429,44	31	29	21	20
AA	17	05/06/2009	422,94	USD	747-400	385	371	193.495,29	31	30	21	21
AA	17	06/03/2009	422,94	USD	747-400	385	246	128.100,22	31	20	21	14
AA	17	07/01/2009	422,94	USD	747-400	385	198	102.728,02	31	16	21	11
AA	17	07/29/2009	422,94	USD	747-400	385	115	59.558,55	31	9	21	7
AA	17	08/26/2009	422,94	USD	747-400	385	70	37.007,28	31	6	21	4

Figure 6.2 Presentation of Data from Persistent Objects in an ALV Grid Control

The conversion of persistent objects into structured tables is identical if you directly use a control, for example, an ALV grid control of the CL_GUI_ALV_GRID class instead of the REUSE_ALV_GRID_DISPLAY function module. Instead of using the internal table as a parameter when you call the function module, in this case, you transfer the internal table to the control directly via the methods with which you assign an output table to the control.

In the previous example, data was displayed in the user interface that existed in the same structure and in the same form in the database. Here the question is justi-fied whether it would make more sense to read the data directly from the database without using Object Services with an Open SQL statement and present the data in the user interface. In fact, the use of Object Services doesn't provide major benefits in a simple case like the one outlined in this example.

But already a little more complex use cases illustrate the benefits of the procedure described: If the presented persistent objects contain transient attributes, you can display them in the user interface without having to manually compose this data after a database query as it would be the case if you did not use Object Services.

If the data for a persistent object doesn't originate from a database table, without Object Services, you would have to compose the data to be presented manually, or you would have to create a view, which brings together the database tables used, in addition to the persistent class. Particularly if you combine the same database tables in different configurations with different database tables, respectively, for instance, in connection with inheritance structures, Object Services help you keep an overview.

Also, if you enable the user to make changes to the data presented in the interface, you benefit from the use of Object Services even more. After you've transferred the changes that the user made to the data presented to the persistent objects, for instance, using the STRUCTURE_TO_OBJECT method, only the actually changed objects are in the CHANGED management state. You can use the Transaction Service to then transfer the changes to the database system in a targeted manner without transferring unchanged objects. You can also use the Transaction Service to undo changes if required without communicating with the database system.

You also automatically benefit from plausibility checks, which you've implemented in the persistent classes, if you use Object Services. Section 7.1, Plausibility Checks, in Chapter 7, describes the various options for the integration of plausibility checks in connection with persistent classes.

6.4.2 Using Persistent Objects in Web Dynpro Contexts

The latest technology for developing user interfaces in ABAP, Web Dynpro ABAP, manages data that is displayed in the user interface and is entered by the user via *contexts*. In a context, the data, which is used in a Web Dynpro component or in a view, is hierarchically stored in nodes and attributes. You can address these nodes and attributes via objects and their methods.

Among the many options to set data in a context or read it from a context, there is none that enables you to transfer a persistent object directly so that its attributes are displayed in the user interface of the application or are even provided for editing. Here, as well, it's only planned that you set and read attributes individually or set or read all attributes in a node via a structure.

If you want to use Object Services in combination with Web Dynpro ABAP, you should store both references to the persistent objects and individual attributes of the persistent objects, which you want to use in the user interface, in the context. By means of the references to the persistent objects, you can call the methods of the persistent objects and read and change their attributes. You need the individual context attributes with the values from the attributes of the persistent objects to be able to assign attributes to the UI elements.

Figure 6.3 shows a reasonable structure to store the references to persistent objects and the individual attributes in a context. With this context, you can manage the flight plan objects of the /IOT/CL_SPFLI class.

A structure from the data dictionary is assigned to the SPFLI context node; this structure contains a component for each attribute of the persistent class. Because in this example the attributes of the persistent class have the same name as the fields of the database table and no transient attributes exist, you can use the SPFLI database table as the type. In some cases, you must possibly revert to an adapted structure. The SPFLI context node is supposed to include any number of flight plans, so it's assigned with the cardinality of 0..N.

The individual components of the assigned structure are subordinate to the SPFLI context node in the form of context attributes. The REFERENCES context node is also subordinate to the SPFLI context node. It contains the RF_SPFLI context attribute in which you can store a reference to the respective persistent flight plan object for each flight plan.

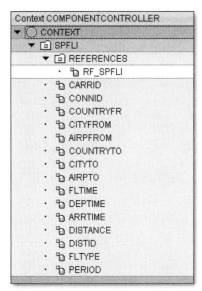

Figure 6.3 Web Dynpro Context for Using Persistent Objects

You should not add the reference to the persistent object together with the attribute that is supposed to be presented and is of the elementary type directly under the same context node. With such an arrangement, it's more difficult to differentiate whether the context attributes are attributes of a persistent object or the reference to a persistent object. Also various automatic assignments aren't possible. For example, you can't assign a context node, to which references are directly appended, via the Create Binding function in a single step to a table in the user interface, as it's otherwise possible via a table's context menu in the View Editor of the development environment for Web Dynpro ABAP.

Listing 6.7 shows how you can fill a context with the structure presented in Figure 6.3. The listing contains a method that is executed before a view is displayed. The method instantiates all flight plans that exist in the system in the form of persistent objects and then fills the context with the values of the persistent objects' attributes. The method also stores the references to the persistent objects in the context.

```
METHOD wddoinit.
  DATA:
    rf_ca_spfli      TYPE REF TO /iot/ca_spfli,
    rf_spfli         TYPE REF TO /iot/cl_spfli,
```

```
        ri_query_manager TYPE REF TO if_os_query_manager,
        ri_query         TYPE REF TO if_os_query,
        ri_node_spfli    TYPE REF TO if_wd_context_node,
        ri_element_spfli TYPE REF TO if_wd_context_element,
        ri_node_refs     TYPE REF TO if_wd_context_node,
        ro_spfli         TYPE REF TO object,
        st_spfli         TYPE if_flight_plan_list=>element_spfli,
        ta_ro_spfli      TYPE osreftab.

    rf_ca_spfli = /iot/ca_spfli=>agent.
    ri_query_manager = cl_os_system=>get_query_manager( ).

*  Instantiate all flight plans that are available in the
*  system via a query with the Query Service
    ri_query = ri_query_manager->create_query( ).
    ta_ro_spfli =
      rf_ca_spfli->if_os_ca_persistency~get_persistent_by_query(
        ri_query ).

*  Request a reference to the SPFLI context node
    ri_node_spfli =
      wd_context->get_child_node( name = wd_this->wdctx_spfli ).

*  For each instantiated flight plan, store the data of the
*  attributes and a reference to the persistent object
*  in the context
    LOOP AT ta_ro_spfli INTO ro_spfli.
*     Typecast: object -> /iot/cl_spfli
      rf_spfli ?= ro_spfli.

*     Transfer the values of the flight plan's attributes
*     to a structure
      CALL METHOD
        /iot/cl_obj_struct_converter=>object_to_structure
        EXPORTING
          im_ro_input  = rf_spfli
        IMPORTING
          ex_st_output = st_spfli.

*     Add the values from structure in a new context element to
*     the SPFLI context node
```

```
      ri_element_spfli =
        ri_node_spfli->bind_structure(
          new_item            = st_spfli
          set_initial_elements = abap_false ).

*    Request a reference to the REFERENCES context node of the
*    previously newly created context element
      ri_node_refs =
        ri_element_spfli->get_child_node(
          wd_this->wdctx_references ).

*    Store a reference to the persistent object in the
*    RF_SPFLI context attribute
      ri_node_refs->set_attribute(
        name  = 'RF_SPFLI'
        value = rf_spfli ).
  ENDLOOP.
ENDMETHOD.
```

Listing 6.7 Using Persistent Objects for Filling a Web Dynpro Context

The method instantiates the flight plans using the Query Service. For this purpose, it uses a query that contains neither filter nor sort conditions. The method stores the data from the query's result below the SPFLI node in the context.

In doing so, it transfers the data from a flight plan object to the ST_SPFLI structure using the previously presented method, OBJECT_TO_STRUCTURE. This structure variable is defined via the structure type of the SPFLI context node. It can therefore be transferred to the BIND_STRUCTURE method directly after filling to pass the values to the individual attributes of the context.

Ultimately, the method shown in Listing 6.7 stores the reference to the persistent object in the context. In this process, it requests a reference to the REFERENCES context node that is subordinate to the SPFLI node. It finally stores the reference to the flight plan in the RF_SPFLI context attribute below this node.

You can use a UI element of the Table type to display the content of the SPFLI context node in the user interface. This way, you can display the flight plans as shown in Figure 6.4.

Airline	Flight Number	Depart.city	Arrival city	Flight time	Departure	Arrival Time	Distance	Distance in
AA	0017	NEW YORK	SAN FRANCISCO	6:01	11:00:00	14:01:00	2,587.0000	MI
AA	0064	SAN FRANCISCO	NEW YORK	5:21	09:00:00	17:21:00	2,572.0000	MI
AZ	0555	ROME	FRANKFURT	2:05	19:00:00	21:05:00	845.0000	MI
AZ	0788	ROME	TOKYO	12:55	12:00:00	08:55:00	6,130.0000	MI
AZ	0789	TOKYO	ROME	15:40	11:45:00	19:25:00	6,130.0000	MI
AZ	0790	ROME	OSAKA	13:35	10:35:00	08:10:00	5,000.0000	MI
DL	0106	NEW YORK	FRANKFURT	7:55	19:35:00	09:30:00	3,851.0000	MI
DL	1699	NEW YORK	SAN FRANCISCO	6:22	17:15:00	20:37:00	2,572.0000	MI
DL	1984	SAN FRANCISCO	NEW YORK	5:25	10:00:00	18:25:00	2,572.0000	MI
JL	0407	TOKYO	FRANKFURT	12:05	13:30:00	17:35:00	9,100.0000	KM
JL	0408	FRANKFURT	TOKYO	11:15	20:25:00	15:40:00	9,100.0000	KM
LH	0400	FRANKFURT	NEW YORK	7:24	10:10:00	11:34:00	6,162.0000	KM
LH	0401	NEW YORK	FRANKFURT	7:15	18:30:00	07:45:00	6,162.0000	KM
LH	0402	FRANKFURT	NEW YORK	7:35	13:30:00	15:05:00	6,162.0000	KM
LH	2402	FRANKFURT	BERLIN	1:05	10:30:00	11:35:00	555.0000	KM

Row 1 of 26

Figure 6.4 Web Dynpro Interface with Flight Plan Data in the Table

6.4.3 Setting the Transaction Mode in a Web Dynpro Application

To use the Transaction Service selectively in a specific transaction mode, you must set the transaction mode before you work with any persistent object. A possible location at which you can integrate the call of the INIT_AND_SET_MODES method with a Web Dynpro application is the WDDOINIT method of the component controller in a Web Dynpro component. The system always calls this method before it displays the first view. In contrast to the WDDOINIT method of a Web Dynpro view, the method in the component controller also provides the benefit that the initialization of the transaction mode is still carried out at the right moment even if you select another initial view for your Web Dynpro application.

Listing 6.8 shows an example for setting the transaction mode within the WDDOINIT method of the component controller.

```
METHOD wddoinit.
* Set the transaction mode:
* The application runs in the object-oriented transaction mode
  cl_os_system=>init_and_set_modes(
    i_external_commit = abap_false ).


* Request a reference to the Transaction Manager
  wd_this->ri_transaction_manager =
    cl_os_system=>get_transaction_manager( ).
```

```
* Create a new transaction and start it as a
* top-level transaction
  wd_this->ri_top_transaction =
    wd_this->ri_transaction_manager->create_transaction( ).
  wd_this->ri_top_transaction->start( ).
ENDMETHOD.
```

Listing 6.8 Listing 6.8 Setting the Transaction Mode Upon Startup of a Web Dynpro Application

In Listing 6.8, the transaction mode is set to the object-oriented transaction mode. Also, the system creates a new transaction and starts it as a top-level transaction. References to the top-level transaction and to the Transaction Manager are stored in attributes of the component controller to be able to access both conveniently at any time.

6.5   Summary

This chapter introduced you to the options to design various, frequently required functions more conveniently. This included general methods for reloading persistent object from the database, removing persistent objects from the management via the Persistency Service, as well as transferring data between persistent objects and structures. For the latter function, the example of the SAP technologies for developing user interfaces showed how you can use the presented methods to use services that can't directly work with persistent objects.

The next chapter will present further possible enhancements of the functions Object Services provide. Among other things, you will learn how to integrate plausibility checks into the access methods of persistent classes.

In real life, it's important to only write meaningful data to objects. This chapter describes how you can ensure that this is adhered to in persistent classes using plausibility checks. You can also use the approaches discussed for further enhancements in persistent classes.

7   Intelligent Persistent Objects

You can implement additional methods in persistent classes in the same way as in usual classes and thus enhance the functionality of the entire class. It isn't that easy, however, to enhance automatically generated implementations of methods in persistent classes with custom functions.

For example, the automatically generated access methods in persistent classes, which you can use to read and change values of attributes, don't contain a logic that checks if the value passed is valid. It's also not possible to simply calculate a return value or trigger further dependent actions during the execution of an access method.

This chapter introduces various approaches that enable you to ensure that the system always carries out user-defined plausibility checks when accessing attributes of persistent objects. Besides plausibility checks, numerous other enhancements are possible that provide persistent objects with functions that go beyond object-relational mapping and make the persistent objects intelligent persistent objects. Using an example of additional enhancements of persistent classes, the chapter describes how you can integrate a lazy loading mechanism with an access method. This kind of mechanism is useful, for instance, if you want to efficiently manage references to associated objects or determine elementary transient attributes only if necessary.

7.1   Plausibility Checks

Plausibility checks are used to ensure that the attributes of persistent objects only adopt valid values. You have to define individually for each attribute which values are valid. For attributes with a Boolean type, for example, `abap_true` and `abap_false` can be the only valid values, and all other values would be invalid. The number of occupied seats for a flight can't adopt a negative value. Within plausibility checks, you can also carry out more complex checks that consider dependencies between several attributes or pieces of data from other persistent classes or database tables. For example, the arrival time of a flight must not be earlier than its departure time, and an aircraft type that is supposed to be used for specific flights must be known in the system.

Unfortunately, the Object Services documentation in the SAP Help Portal doesn't contain any descriptions of appropriate approaches for enhancing access methods of attributes of persistent classes with plausibility checks. To address this, we discuss various variants for the integration of plausibility checks and compare the advantages and disadvantages of these variants.

You can use one of the following four variants to enhance the methods for accessing attributes of persistent objects with plausibility checks:

▶ You implement the plausibility checks in the persistent class in custom access methods whose names do *not* begin with `GET_` or `SET_`.

▶ In addition to the persistent class, you create a usual class with access methods. You then implement the plausibility checks in the usual class and delegate the management of the attributes to the persistent class.

▶ You create a persistent subclass for a persistent class. You redefine the access methods in the subclass and thereby add plausibility checks.

▶ You include the plausibility checks in the access methods in the persistent class using the Enhancement Framework.

Warning: Automatic Generation of Access Methods

Don't directly modify the generated access methods in the persistent class. The Persistence Service always overwrites these methods automatically and without warning when you modify the persistence representation or attributes of a persistent class. Plausibility checks and other enhancements that you've implemented in the access methods get lost during this process.

7.1.1 Variant 1: Custom Access Methods with Different Names in the Persistent Class

To enhance persistent classes with plausibility checks, you can create new methods in the persistent class. These methods are used to access the attributes of the persistent objects. Because the automated source code generation of the Persistence Service doesn't overwrite methods that you've created yourself, you can implement plausibility checks in these methods, and these checks are then retained permanently.

Because you can't create methods that begin with the GET_ or SET_ prefix in persistent classes yourself, you have to assign the names for the custom methods according to a schema that is different from the schema used by the Persistence Service. In real life, experience has shown that it's quite complex and error-prone if you define specific access methods solely for attributes that were enhanced with further functions. Although the creation of the class initially involves more implementation work, you should always use custom access methods for the access to all attributes right from the beginning if you decide to work with the variant described here.

Figure 7.1 shows a class diagram with possible attributes resulting from this procedure. In the persistent class, /IOT/CL_SBOOK, all attributes and consequently all automatically generated access methods are defined with the Private visibility. Accordingly, external access to the attributes of the class is only possible via the manually implemented methods with the Public visibility. They begin with the READ_ or WRITE_ prefixes here. This ensures that no user of the persistent class can bypass the plausibility checks and enter invalid values for the attributes. Because every read access is implemented via a manually created method, you can also enhance the automatically generated functionality for read access according to your requirements.

To not bypass the mechanisms that the Persistence Service provides, you should use the generated access methods (see Listing 7.1) rather than accessing the attributes directly in the manually created access methods.

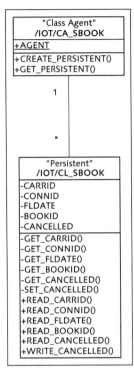

Figure 7.1 Class Diagram of the Integration of Plausibility Checks via Custom Access Methods

```abap
METHOD write_cancelled.
* Check if a valid value was passed
  IF im_cancelled <> abap_false AND im_cancelled <> abap_true.
*    An invalid value was passed,
*    abort execution
    RETURN.
  ENDIF.

* Change the value of the CANCELLED attribute
* using the respective access method
  me->set_cancelled( im_cancelled ).
ENDMETHOD.
```

Listing 7.1 Plausibility Check in a Manually Created Method of a Persistent Class

The `WRITE_CANCELLED` method enables the calling program to modify the `CAN-CELLED` attribute of a flight booking. This attribute specifies if the respective flight booking has been canceled. The only permitted values are therefore `abap_true` and `abap_false`. The `WRITE_CANCELLED` method terminates further processing if the calling program passes a different value. If the value passed is valid, the method writes this value to the attribute of the persistent object using the automatically generated access method, `SET_CANCELLED`.

Because you can create a method like `WRITE_CANCELLED` yourself and define the method's parameter interface, you can also provide the calling program with additional information. For example, you can use a return value to notify the calling program if the value passed was valid and thus written to the attribute. You can also declare an exception in the method definition and trigger this exception in the method if the calling program passes an invalid value.

7.1.2 Variant 2: Delegation with Access Methods in a Usual Class

The second variant for the integration of persistent objects and plausibility checks strictly separates object-relational mapping and application logic. Persistent classes only manage the functions that the automatically generated part of the persistent class provides. Enhancements, such as plausibility checks, are supposed to be included in an additional usual class.

For this variant, applications solely work with the objects of the usual class; they don't directly access objects of the persistent class. You should therefore assign a compact, meaningful name to the usual class, and also select a name based on it for the persistent class, for example, by adding the `_PERSISTENT` suffix.

Figure 7.2 illustrates the proposed structure using the flight booking as an example. The persistent class, `/IOT/CL_SBOOK_PERSISTENT`, and the corresponding class agent exclusively contain ABAP source code for object-relational mapping, which the Persistence Service generates automatically. The usual class, `/IOT/CL_SBOOK`, contains the plausibility checks and more manually created enhancements. Every object of the usual class includes a reference to the respective object of the persistent class to be able to forward accesses to attributes.

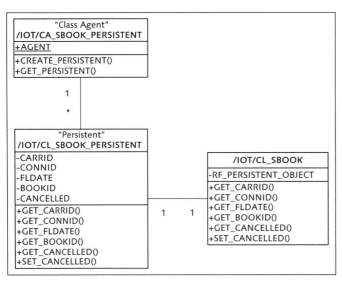

Figure 7.2 Class Diagram of the Integration of Plausibility Checks via Delegation

Listing 7.2 shows how the implementation of the access method for the CAN-
CELLED attribute can be structured. The SET_CANCELLED method in the usual class
first checks if the value passed is valid. If the value is invalid, further processing
is aborted. If the value passed is valid, it calls the corresponding method of the
persistent class and thus delegates the task of permanently storing the new value
to the persistent object.

```
METHOD set_cancelled.
* Check if a valid value was passed
  IF im_cancelled <> abap_false AND im_cancelled <> abap_true.
*    An invalid value was passed,
*    abort execution
    RETURN.
  ENDIF.

* Change the value of the CANCELLED attribute in the
* persistent object using the respective access method
  me->rf_persistent_object->set_cancelled( im_cancelled ).
ENDMETHOD.
```

Listing 7.2 Plausibility Check in a Manually Created Method of a Persistent Class

This variant for the integration of plausibility checks also enables you to declare additional parameters or exceptions in the method's parameter interface and use them in the method.

Besides the access methods in the usual class, you also have to implement the management of the objects of the usual class when using this variant. You should ensure that the application doesn't work with various objects of the usual class to access the same persistent object. To implement such behavior, you must reproduce some of the functions of the class agent of a persistent class for your usual class.

This variant involves additional effort because you have to implement access methods in the usual class for any attribute, even if you don't want to enhance the corresponding automatically generated method of the persistent class with additional functions.

7.1.3   Variant 3: Persistent Subclass

The third variant also distributes implementations of object-relational mapping and plausibility checks across two classes. The class with the plausibility checks is a subclass of the persistent class in which you implement the persistence representation, which means that it's a persistent class itself. In the subclass, you redefine the access methods that you want to enhance with plausibility checks.

Figure 7.3 illustrates the resulting structure for the flight booking sample. Here again, the class that is supposed to be used by the applications has the compact, meaningful name /IOT/CL_SBOOK. The name of the persistent superclass has the _OR_MAPPING suffix to indicate that only object-relational mapping is defined here.

The SET_CANCELLED method from Listing 7.3 is an example of a redefinition of a method in the persistent subclass, /IOT/CL_SBOOK. Like the methods from previous listings, this method also first checks if the passed parameter has a valid value. If the value is invalid, further processing is aborted. If the calling program passes a valid value, the method uses the passed value to call the automatically generated access method in the superclass using the super pseudo reference. The access method then writes the value to the attribute of the persistent object.

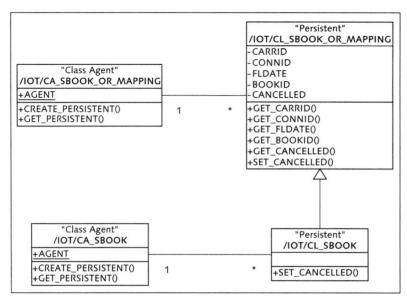

Figure 7.3 Class Diagram of the Integration of Plausibility Checks via Inheritance

```
METHOD set_cancelled.
* Check if a valid value was passed
  IF i_cancelled <> abap_false AND i_cancelled <> abap_true.
*    An invalid value was passed,
*    abort execution
    RETURN.
  ENDIF.

* Change the value of the CANCELLED attribute
* using the respective access method of the superclass
  super->set_cancelled( i_cancelled ).
ENDMETHOD.
```

Listing 7.3 Plausibility Check in a Persistent Subclass

In contrast to the two variants described before, the method's parameter interface is already defined for this variant. The Persistence Service defines it in the superclass during the automatic generation. In redefinitions of these methods, the parameter interface always corresponds to the parameter interface of the respective method in the superclass. This means that you can't define your own exception classes. You also can't freely select the name of the importing parameter or add more parameters. In Listing 7.3, the only parameter's name has been automatically defined by the Persistence Service to be I_CANCELLED and not IM_CANCELLED as in the previous listings.

For this variant, the implementation effort is rather low. You only have to create the persistent subclass and then, in this class, redefine the methods that will be provided with additional functions. All other methods of the originally persistent class are automatically available in the subclass due to the inheritance mechanism.

7.1.4 Variant 4: Enhancement Framework

The fourth variant for the integration of plausibility checks in persistent classes isn't only based on the common components of object-oriented software development, it also uses the Enhancement Framework to enhance the application logic of the generated access methods directly without changing the ABAP source code of the method. One of the prerequisites for this variant is SAP NetWeaver AS ABAP Release 7.0 because the Enhancement Framework isn't available in earlier releases.

Excursus: Enhancement Framework

The Enhancement Framework enables you to enhance repository objects — that is, both data dictionary objects and ABAP source code — without changing the original repository object. The Enhancement Framework is supposed to replace previous enhancement technologies, such as the Modification Assistant, customer exits, and Business Add-Ins (BAdIs).

A position in the ABAP source code where you can enhance the existing application logic is called an enhancement option. You distinguish between implicit and explicit enhancement options:

- Implicit enhancement options are automatically provided at specific positions in the ABAP source code, for example, at the beginning and at the end of each method.

- Explicit enhancement options, in contrast, can exist anywhere in a method. You have to explicitly create explicit enhancement options during the development of the original ABAP source code to identify an additional position where the application logic can be enhanced.

The ABAP source code with which you enhance the original ABAP source code is called an enhancement or synonymously an enhancement implementation.

To integrate plausibility checks into an access method of a persistent class, you should use the implicit enhancement option at the beginning of the access method that you want to enhance. Here, you can integrate an enhancement that checks the passed parameter before the original method is executed. For the integration of plausibility checks with the Enhancement Framework, you don't have to create new methods or new classes.

Therefore, the class diagram in Figure 7.4 is identical to a class diagram that shows a persistent class and the corresponding class agent without plausibility checks.

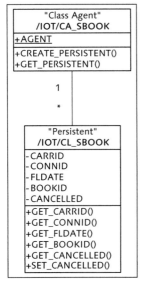

Figure 7.4 Class Diagram of the Integration of Plausibility Checks with the Enhancement Framework

You need to perform the following steps to enhance an access method of a persistent class with plausibility checks:

1. Have the Class Builder display the source code of the method that you want to enhance.

2. Change to the enhancement mode using the Enhance button, the Ctrl + F4 key combination, or the METHOD • ENHANCE menu entry.

3. To enhance an implicit enhancement option, the implicit enhancement options need to be visible. This can be done via the EDIT • ENHANCEMENT OPERATIONS • SHOW IMPLICIT ENHANCEMENT OPTIONS menu entry.

4. Place the cursor on the line with the implicit enhancement option at the beginning of the method. In the access methods of persistent classes, this is the second

line of the method's source code (see Figure 7.5). Use the EDIT • ENHANCEMENT
OPERATIONS • CREATE ENHANCEMENT menu entry to create an enhancement. If
the system prompts the enhancement type, select Code.

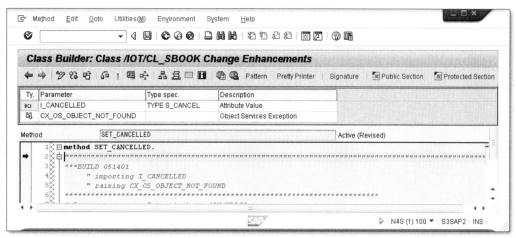

Figure 7.5 An Implicit Enhancement Option

5. In the dialog box that appears for the creation of the enhancement (see Figure 7.6), enter a name for the enhancement and a descriptive short text. The name must lie in the customer namespace (first letter: Y or Z) or in a namespace you've reserved, as is the case for any other repository object. You don't have to make any specifications in the Composite Enhancement Implementation input field.

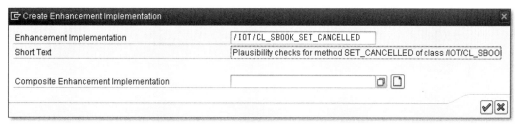

Figure 7.6 Dialog Box for the Creation of Enhancements

6. You can now implement the plausibility checks or any other ABAP source code between the ENHANCEMENT and ENDENHANCEMENT statements. All other statements that you use in the ENHANCEMENT block have the same effects as if they were

implemented at the position of the implicit enhancement option in the ABAP source code of the original method. As a result, you can use RETURN to exit the method, for example, or the me self-reference to access attributes or methods of the persistent object.

7. To make your changes take effect, you must save and activate the enhancement.

Listing 7.4 shows a sample implementation of an enhancement. Again, the value that was passed to the SET_CANCELLED method must be checked to make sure it's valid. If the value is invalid, the RETURN statement ensures that not only the enhancement but also the method is exited. If the value is valid, no further action must be taken within the enhancement. Because the enhancement of the implicit enhancement option was implemented at the beginning of the access method, the original method is still executed after the enhancement.

```
ENHANCEMENT 1 /IOT/CL_SBOOK_SET_CANCELLED.
* Check if a valid value was passed
  IF i_cancelled <> abap_false AND i_cancelled <> abap_true.
*    An invalid value was passed,
*    abort execution
    RETURN.
  ENDIF.
ENDENHANCEMENT.
```

Listing 7.4 Plausibility Check in an Enhancement Using the Enhancement Framework

The specific integration of enhancements in ABAP source code using the Enhancement Framework also affects the display of the source code in the various development environment tools:

▸ The Class Builder displays the source code of the enhancement directly at the position of the implicit enhancement option (see Figure 7.7). This view also enables you to edit the enhancement.

▸ The ABAP Debugger displays the original method and the enhancement separately. The view of the original method, in contrast, neither displays the implicit enhancement options nor the ABAP source code of the enhancement. Only the helical enhancement icon on the left of the ABAP Debugger indicates where the method has been enhanced (see Figure 7.8).

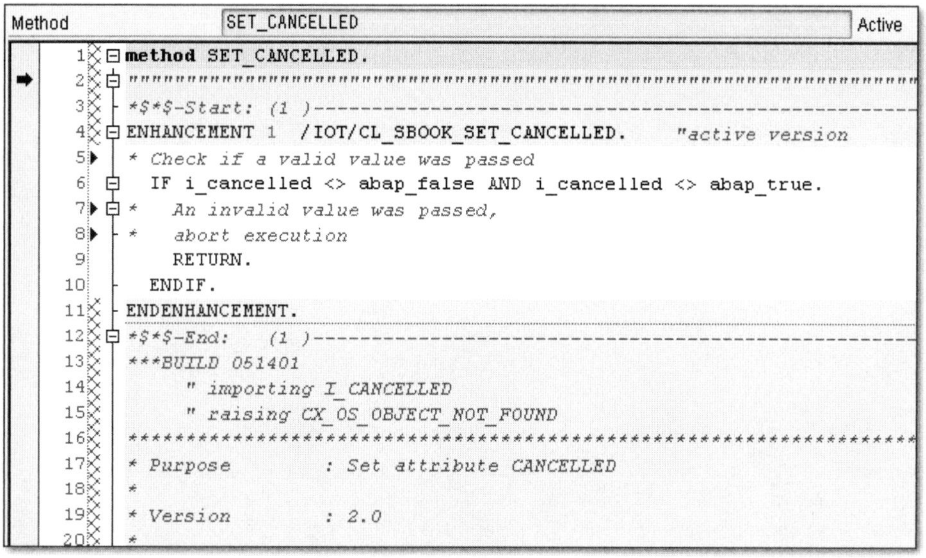

Figure 7.7 Editing an Enhancement in the Class Builder

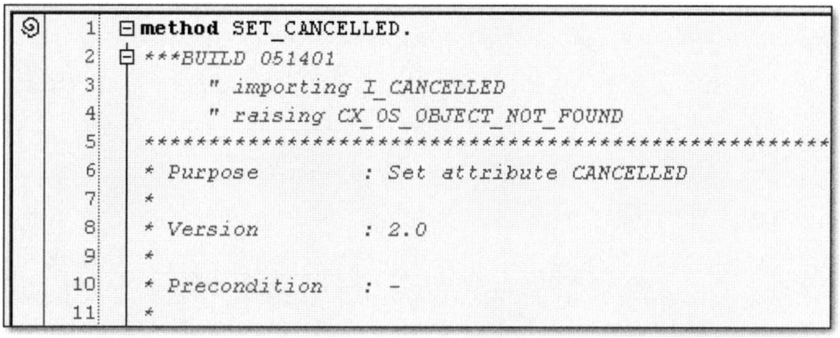

Figure 7.8 Presentation of an Enhanced Original Method in the ABAP Debugger

The ABAP Debugger displays the ABAP source code of the enhancement similarly to a method (see Figure 7.9). The enhancement is mapped as a separate line in the ABAP stack. However, because it isn't a hierarchical level in the traditional sense, the enhancement is indicated by a special stack type. Also, the enhancement has the same stack depth as the enhanced original method (see Figure 7.10).

```
1  ⊟ ENHANCEMENT 1  .
2  |  * Check if a valid value was passed
3  ⊟|  IF i_cancelled <> abap_false AND i_cancelled <> abap_true.
4  ⊟*    An invalid value was passed,
5  ├ *    abort execution
6        RETURN.
7  ├    ENDIF.
8  └ ENDENHANCEMENT.
```

Figure 7.9 Presentation of an Enhancement in the ABAP Debugger

ABAP Stack						
Sta...	Stac...	S...	Event Type	Event	Program	Nav...
⇨	46	⊚	METHOD	SET_CANCELLED	/IOT/CL_SBOOK=======	▤
	46	▤	METHOD	SET_CANCELLED	/IOT/CL_SBOOK=======	▤
	45	▤	FORM	%_SET_CANCELLED	%_T01B81	▤
	44	▤	FUNCTION	SETS_FA_METHOD_INVO	SAPLSETF	▤

Figure 7.10 Enhancement in the ABAP Stack of the ABAP Debugger

If you use the proposed variant for the integration of plausibility checks in the access methods of persistent classes via the Enhancement Framework, you enhance the automatically generated access methods. The method's parameter interface is therefore already defined. You can't define your own parameters or additional exception classes.

At first glance, the introduced variant seems to be an unusual use case of the Enhancement Framework because the customer doesn't enhance the SAP source code, but a developer enhances the methods of a class that he has created himself. But in fact, the SAP Enhancement Framework is designed to enable developers to enhance their own source code and activate or deactivate the enhancements or replace them with other enhancements without having to adapt the original source code.

7.1.5 Comparing the Various Variants

Unfortunately, none of the four variants introduced provides major benefits that justify a recommendation without any restrictions. Table 7.1 summarizes the effects the individual variants have.

Variant	Interfaces of the Methods	Implementation Effort	Calling Program Uses...	Available as of Release
1	Freely definable	Medium	The same class, different method names	6.10
2	Freely definable	High	A different class, the same method names	6.10
3	Predefined	Low	A different class, the same method names	6.10
4	Predefined	Low	The same class, the same method names	7.0

Table 7.1 Overview of the Advantages and Disadvantages of the Various Variants for the Integration of Plausibility Checks

▶ If you work with variant 1, you have to create the access methods for each attribute manually. This gives you the flexibility to freely define the method's interface, but the effort for manually implementing all methods separately and always maintaining all adaptations is immense. The calling program benefits from being still able to work with the objects of the persistent class but isn't allowed to use the methods whose names begin with the GET_ and SET_ prefixes.

▶ The most apparent characteristic of variant 2 is the implementation effort, which is significantly larger than for all other variants. In variant 1, you have to write specific access methods for every attribute; here, you also have to develop the management of objects of the usual class that are used by the applications in this variant. The large amount of effort is rewarded with maximum flexibility for designing the methods and their interfaces and also results in a software architecture with a clear separation of concerns: The application logic is implemented in the usual class, and the object-relational mapping is implemented in the persistent class. However, the advantages can hardly compensate the disadvantage of the high level of implementation effort.

▶ Variant 3 involves considerably less effort because you only need to create a subclass of an existing class. Also, you only have to redefine the access methods that you want to enhance with additional functions. Two persistent classes are involved, but the applications can continue to work with a single persistent class, the corresponding class agent, and the access methods with the GET_ and SET_ prefixes in the name.

However, because of the two persistent classes, there is the danger that applications will use the objects of the superclass and thus write invalid values to the persistent attributes. Also, this variant combines different interpretations of inheritance relationship semantics. In this variant, an inheritance relationship can stand for a mere technical process, which is required for the integration of the logic. Of course, it can also be a content-motivated specialization, for example, for flights that are categorized into charter flights and scheduled flights. The resulting software architecture is complex because the two different types of inheritance relationships can't be distinguished at first glance, and the inheritance depth and consequently the number of persistent classes and class agents doubles. You can't adapt the parameter interfaces of the access methods.

▶ For variant 4, the implementation effort is low as well. Here, you only have to implement the enhancements that you want to include in the access methods. You can't adapt the parameter interfaces of the access methods. Variant 4 is the only variant in which only one persistent class exists and in which the calling program can directly call the generated methods of the persistent class. However, you have to live with the current restrictions of the Enhancement Framework, for example, for the Refactoring Tools and the Pretty Printer. You also have to get used to the different ways in which the Class Builder and particularly the ABAP Debugger show the enhancements. A prerequisite for variant 4 is SAP NetWeaver AS ABAP Release 7.0.

In current releases, the goal of being able to access persistent objects, which contain plausibility checks or other enhancements, from the application as usual without a great deal of implementation effort can be reached best if you work with the Enhancement Framework and variant 4. However, due to the mentioned restrictions, it may be useful or necessary to use one of the other variants.

7.2 Lazy Loading

Not only can you use the variants for enhancing access methods described in Section 7.1, Plausibility Checks, to implement plausibility checks but you can also implement any other enhancement for access methods. The approaches described enable you to enhance both SET methods and GET methods. For the different enhancements, the advantages and disadvantages of the various approaches can emerge very differently. For example, it can make sense to use a different variant for plausibility checks than for triggering an event when accessing an attribute.

This section describes how you can use a lazy loading mechanism to manage references to any number of objects in an attribute of a persistent class. This function can't be implemented via the persistent references that are automatically managed by the Persistence Service. If an attribute is defined as a persistence reference, you can only reference a single persistent object using this attribute.

The basic idea of the lazy loading design pattern is to only determine data when it's actually required. The data then remains stored in the object so that it doesn't have to be redetermined if the object is accessed again. This way, you avoid both loading data that isn't required at all and loading the same data multiple times. Without lazy loading, there is the danger of triggering a chain reaction upon the instantiation of an object as described in Section 2.4, Persistent References, in Chapter 2. A management of references to objects via lazy loading enables you to provide comfortable and simultaneously efficient access to the referenced objects for users of a persistent object.

Listing 7.5 contains an example of the implementation of a lazy loading mechanism through the Enhancement Framework (see Section 7.1.4, Variant 4: Enhancement Framework). In the persistent class of the flight plan, every object should contain references to all flights with the respective flight plan in a transient attribute called TA_RF_FLIGHTS. In Listing 7.5, the GET_TA_RF_FLIGHTS access method is enhanced so that it determines all flights for the flight plan via the database upon first access. For all subsequent accesses, the method then returns the already determined flights.

```
ENHANCEMENT 1  /IOT/CL_SPFLI_GET_TA_RF_FLIGHT.
  DATA: rf_ca_sflight    TYPE REF TO /iot/ca_sflight,
        rf_flight        TYPE REF TO /iot/cl_sflight,
        ri_query_manager TYPE REF TO if_os_query_manager,
        ri_query         TYPE REF TO if_os_query,
        ro_flight        TYPE REF TO object,
        ta_ro_flights    TYPE osreftab,
        v_carrid         TYPE s_carr_id,
        v_connid         TYPE s_conn_id.
```

```
* Have the flights been loaded yet?
  IF me->a_flights_loaded = abap_false.

*    Create query that loads all flights for the flight plan
     ri_query_manager = cl_os_system=>get_query_manager( ).
     ri_query =
       ri_query_manager->create_query(
         i_filter = 'CARRID = PAR1 AND CONNID = PAR2' ).

*    Determine airline and flight number
     v_carrid = me->get_carrid( ).
     v_connid = me->get_connid( ).

*    Execute query with current airline and
*    current flight number
     rf_ca_sflight = /iot/ca_sflight=>agent.
     ta_ro_flights =
      rf_ca_sflight->if_os_ca_persistency~get_persistent_by_query(
         i_query = ri_query
         i_par1  = v_carrid
         i_par2  = v_connid ).

*    Perform typecast of OBJECT to /IOT/CL_SFLIGHT
*    for all instantiated flights and add flight
*    to the internal table in the TA_RF_FLIGHTS attribute
     LOOP AT ta_ro_flights INTO ro_flight.
       rf_flight ?= ro_flight.
       APPEND rf_flight TO me->ta_rf_flights.
     ENDLOOP.

*    Indicate in the A_FLIGHTS_LOADED attribute that
*    flights have already been loaded
     me->a_flights_loaded = abap_true.
   ENDIF.
ENDENHANCEMENT.
```

Listing 7.5 Enhancing an Access Method with a Lazy Loading Mechanism

The enhancement shown in Listing 7.5 is integrated at the beginning of the GET_
TA_RF_FLIGHTS access method through an implicit enhancement option. Before the
automatically generated original method accesses the TA_RF_FLIGHTS attribute, the
enhancement first checks if it has already loaded the flights. If so, the enhancement

has nothing to do, and the original method can return the flights from the attribute. If the enhancement hasn't loaded the flights yet, it loads the flights before the original method is executed. This way, the original method also returns the flights for the flight plan as a result in this case.

To load the flights, the enhancement works with a query using the Query Service. The filter condition of the query includes criteria for the airline and flight number. Using the class agent of the flight class, the enhancement loads all flights from the database that meet the filter condition of the query. Because the query returns an internal table with lines of the OBJECT reference type, but the TA_RF_FLIGHTS attribute expects references to flights, a downcasting is respectively implemented for each object before the enhancement fills the attribute. Finally, in the private attribute A_FLIGHTS_LOADED, the enhancement stores the information that it has loaded the flights. When the method is called the next time, the enhancement can use the attribute to reliably determine whether the flights have already been determined even if no flights exist for the flight plan.

If you use the IF_OS_FACTORY~REFRESH_PERSISTENT method of the class agent to have the Persistence Service load the attributes of a persistent object from the database upon the next access, this initially only affects the persistent attributes of the objects. Listing 7.6 shows how you can also reset the transient attributes that have been used previously. This also ensures that the flights for the flight plan are newly determined from the database when the access method is called the next time.

```
METHOD if_os_state~invalidate.
* Clear references to flights for flight plan
  CLEAR me->ta_rf_flights.

* Reset attribute that indicates whether the references
* to flights for flight plan have already been loaded
  me->a_flights_loaded = abap_false.
ENDMETHOD.
```

Listing 7.6 Resetting Transient Attributes

The Persistence Service calls the IF_OS_STATE~INVALIDATE method of an object before it resets the persistent attributes. The automatic source code generation doesn't overwrite the method. You can therefore modify the method and ensure in the method that the transient attributes are also reset in an appropriate manner.

7.3   Summary

This chapter introduced the different variants for enhancing persistent classes with application logic. The described variants also enable you to integrate plausibility checks with persistent classes and automatically fill transient attributes when the respective attribute is accessed for the first time.

You can also use these variants to integrate any other functions. For example, when attributes are accessed in a specific way, you can trigger events that notify other objects that the attribute has been accessed or that a value has been changed.

In the following chapter, we will describe how you can integrate the SAP Lock Concept with Object Services. The approach we propose enables you to completely automate the SAP Lock Concept in your applications.

You must use the SAP Lock Concept in every application that may be used by multiple users, or in other words, in every application in ABAP. Fortunately, it's possible to integrate the SAP Lock Concept with Object Services so that it's automatically used by every application without additional development work.

8   Integration of the SAP Lock Concept and Object Services

On a SAP NetWeaver AS ABAP, many users can work concurrently, and every user can start multiple applications in parallel. In fact, it's common for multiple users to want to process the same objects at the same time. Currently, Object Services don't include any integrated mechanism that automatically prevents simultaneous modifications to the same objects. If you don't enhance your application with such a mechanism, this can result in undesirable inconsistencies in the system.

For example, if two users use Object Services in applications to implement parallel bookings for the same flight in the flight data model, the internal session of each user initially loads the current flight object from the database. If the flight object states that there is still a seat available, the two users create a new booking. To keep the number of available seats of a flight up-to-date, each of the two internal sessions reduces the number of free seats from 1 to 0. The two users aren't notified that another booking was implemented at the same time. Two bookings are created in the system, although only one free seat was left. Because now more bookings for the flight exist in the system than seats are available on the plane, the flight is now overbooked unintentionally.

Errors like this can occur as soon as two internal sessions run in parallel in the system. The more users work in the system, the higher the probability that two or even more internal sessions process the same objects at the same time. With the SAP Lock Concept, in each SAP NetWeaver AS ABAP, you're provided with a service with which you can prevent concurrent accesses to the same objects.

Errors that result from an incorrect use of a lock concept are among those errors that are most difficult to reproduce and thus most difficult to resolve in software development. It therefore makes sense to use an already proven reusable implementation instead of implementing the access to the SAP Lock Concept for each application again.

This chapter describes how you can integrate the SAP Lock Concept with Object Services. With the implementation presented, you enhance a persistent class so that all users of the persistent class automatically work with the SAP Lock Concept without having to manually set the locks.

8.1   The SAP Lock Concept

The SAP Lock Concept is a service with which you can ensure at application level that two internal sessions can never modify the same object at the same time. Consequently, it differs from lock concepts that are designed to synchronize the accesses to data records at the database level.

Compared to the SAP Lock Concept, locks at the database level have the benefit that the database system uses and manages them fully automatically if a corresponding isolation level is set. Locks at the database level are reliable and well suited for applications that implement certain changes immediately after reading an object without interacting with the user and write the modified object directly to the database. Locks at the database level aren't suited for applications in which users work with objects.

If a user edits an object, a lock must be set at the database level from the time of loading the object until the time of writing the modified object to the database. While this lock is set and the system waits for the actions of the user, other users can't access the edited object — not even in read-only mode. To prevent that such wait situations occur, SAP NetWeaver AS ABAP automatically terminates the running database LUW as soon as an application waits for a user input. Therefore, you need to use a mechanism for synchronizing concurrent accesses to objects at the application level. Such a mechanism is provided by the SAP Lock Concept.

In every SAP system, an enqueue work process is responsible for managing the locks set. As shown in Figure 8.1, in an SAP system with multiple application servers, only one application server, the central instance, includes an enqueue work process. Alternatively, it's possible to set up a server that doesn't fulfill any other tasks except for managing locks. Such a server is referred to as a standalone enqueue server and includes no further work processes besides the enqueue work process.

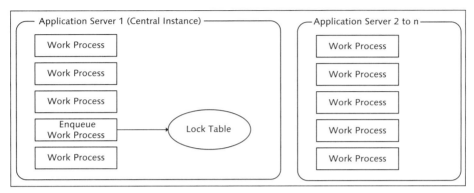

Figure 8.1   Architecture of the SAP Lock Concept

The enqueue work process manages the locks set in the main memory in the lock table. If a work process that wants to set a lock doesn't run on the same server on which the enqueue work process runs, it communicates with the server that is responsible for managing the locks in case it wants to set a lock. This way, it's ensured that — when setting further locks — all work processes across all application servers in an SAP system take account of an already set lock.

The SAP Lock Concept has no direct connection to the database, so you can also set locks for objects that don't exist in the database. For example, you can lock objects in advance that you want to create to prevent someone else in another internal session from creating an object with the same key at the same time.

> **Important: All Applications Must Use the SAP Lock Concept**
>
> Even if the term *lock* implies something else, setting the lock doesn't prevent another internal session from working with same objects as you do. If another internal session in the same system works with an application that doesn't work with the SAP Lock Concept, it can modify objects without opposition for which you've set locks.
>
> To ensure that the SAP Lock Concept works, all applications in a SAP system must explicitly use the SAP Lock Concept. Initially, you must try to set a lock before you process an object. If setting the lock fails, another internal session is already processing the same object. In this case, the application must cancel the processing of the object or try to set locks later before it processes the object.

Using a lock object in the data dictionary for a group of similar objects, you determine with which lock parameters you set the locks. In the context of Object Services, you should usually create one lock object for each persistent class. If you use persistent classes between which inheritance relationships exist, you should respectively create a lock object for the top-most persistent class that isn't defined as abstract. The lock argument should correspond to the key of the persistent object or to the primary key of the underlying database table.

To set a lock from an application using the SAP Lock Concept, you must call a specific function module that is called a lock module. A *lock module* either sets the desired lock or sends a classic exception to the calling program informing it that the lock couldn't be set. In doing so, the lock module addresses the enqueue work process. If the enqueue work process isn't on the same application server as the running internal session, the lock module automatically communicates with the server that provides the enqueue work process.

The system automatically creates lock modules for each defined lock object. The names of the lock modules for setting locks begin with the ENQUEUE_ prefix; the names of the lock modules for manually removing your own locks begin with the DEQUEUE_ prefix. This is followed by the name of the lock object.

To set a lock for a persistent object, you can call the lock module of the lock object that you've created for the persistent class and, in doing so, transfer the key of the persistent object. In all applications that work with the objects of the same class, you should work with the same lock object. You should also use the same lock object if you process the content of a database table in different applications both via Object Services and via classic Open SQL statements.

Listing 8.1 shows an example of a lock module call. In this listing, the lock module for the ESSPFLI lock object is used to set a lock for a flight plan. Via the carrid and connid parameters, the system transfers the key of the flight plan that is supposed to be locked to the lock module. Moreover, the lock mode is transferred to the function module via the mode_spfli parameter (see Section 8.2.1, Lock Mode). If the lock module can't set the required lock, a classic exception is raised. In this case, the application must cancel the processing of the flight plan and possibly try to set the lock later.

```
CALL FUNCTION 'ENQUEUE_ESSPFLI'
  EXPORTING
    mode_spfli     = 'E'
    carrid         = 'AA'
    connid         = 17
  EXCEPTIONS
    foreign_lock   = 1
    system_failure = 2
    OTHERS         = 3.
IF sy-subrc <> 0.
* Error handling: abort processing
  ...
ENDIF.
```

Listing 8.1 Calling a Lock Module

If you don't remove the set locks manually, the locks usually remain set until the end of an SAP LUW, that is, until the end of a top-level transaction. When you set a lock, you can use the optional parameter called _SCOPE to specify that the lock remains set until you end the internal session. The following descriptions respectively refer to locks for which no special specifications were transferred via the _SCOPE parameter.

Note: Automatic Removal of Locks

If you reset an SAP LUW, that is, if you either call the UNDO method of the top-level transaction in the object-oriented transaction mode or use the ROLLBACK WORK statement in the compatibility mode, the system automatically removes all locks that you've set in the same internal session using the _SCOPE = 2 parameter.

However, if you conclude an SAP LUW by calling the END method on the top-level transaction or using the COMMIT WORK statement, the system only removes the locks if an update module is registered. Object Services only register an update module if you haven't selected Direct Update as the update mode and actually modified persistent objects. If you haven't registered any further update modules and work in the Direct Update mode, or if you haven't modified a persistent object, locks which you've set using the _SCOPE = 2 parameter remain set also after completion of the SAP LUW.

With this behavior, you don't run the risk of inconsistencies because the SAP Lock Concept wouldn't apply, but the locks possibly would be set too long, which would unnecessarily restrict the parallel working in the system.

8.2   Pessimistic and Optimistic Locking

A locking strategy is a procedure that describes in which sequence you must set locks with which lock mode to effectively protect your system against inconsistencies caused by concurrent accesses to the same objects. The following sections describe the two different locking strategies that you can implement using the SAP Lock Concept: pessimistic locking and optimistic locking.

▶ The name of the pessimistic locking strategy is based on the assumption that it's very likely that a conflict situation arises while you execute an action with an object. Before you start an action in this locking strategy, you must ensure that no other internal session already executes an action that modifies an object you want to modify. If there's a conflict, you don't even start to carry out the action.

▶ In the optimistic locking strategy, however, you already start the action before you've checked whether conflict situations could arise. This process is based on the hope that no conflict will arise. You only ensure that no concurrent access occurs or has already occurred when you want to write the changes to the database. If you then determine a conflict, you must undo the changes that you've already made in the main memory.

8.2.1   Lock Mode

The lock mode is a property of a set lock and a parameter of the lock modules at the same time. The lock mode decides whether different internal sessions may set locks for the same object at the same time and how the locks affect the other locks already set.

For the subsequently used lock modes, Table 8.1 provides an overview of the prerequisites that must be met so that you can set a lock in a specific lock mode. Moreover, the table indicates the effects that a successful call of a lock module has if you p a specific lock mode.

You should always set exclusive locks if you change already-existing data in the database. Because of this, exclusive locks are also referred to as write locks. The SAP Lock Concept ensures that a maximum of one internal session holds an exclusive lock for an object at any time. If another internal session requests an exclusive lock for an object for which a different internal session already holds a lock with any lock mode, the lock module doesn't set a new lock and returns an exception.

Lock Mode	Prerequisite	Effects
E (exclusive)	No other internal session holds a lock with any other lock mode for the same object.	Lock is set in the lock mode E.
O (optimistic)	No other internal session holds an exclusive lock for the same object.	Lock is set in the lock mode O.
R (conversion)	Own internal session holds an optimistic lock for the object.	A lock in the lock mode O becomes a lock in lock mode E; all locks of other internal sessions for the same object in the lock mode O are removed.

Table 8.1 Overview of the Lock Modes Used

By means of optimistic locks, you can check whether another internal session has modified a specific object since you've set your optimistic lock. Multiple internal sessions can respectively hold an optimistic lock for the same object at the same time. You can convert an optimistic lock into an exclusive lock. If other internal sessions hold optimistic locks for the same object at the time of the conversion, these are removed. Optimistic locks are thus the only locks that — once they have been set — can't just disappear when you terminate the SAP LUW or the internal session or when you call the lock modules for removing locks. If an internal session tries to convert its optimistic lock after this lock has been removed by the conversion of another internal session, the conversion fails with an exception.

An internal session can never hold an optimistic lock while another internal session holds an exclusive lock. A successful conversion of a lock therefore always implies that no other internal session holds an exclusive lock for the same object.

8.2.2 Pessimistic Locking

The pessimistic locking strategy ensures that only one internal session processes an object at the same time. If another internal session wants to process the same object, it can't do so until the internal session that processes the object has concluded the processing of the object.

Figure 8.2 shows a UML sequence diagram with the individual steps of pessimistic locking. You first set an exclusive lock for the object you want to work with. Only then do you load the object from the database, modify the object, and then write the modifications to the database by finishing the top-level transaction.

Particularly in the context of Object Services, you must ensure that you have to load the object from the database *after* the lock is set. If you load the object in the same internal session as previously and then request the class agent again to instantiate the same object, the class agent doesn't load the object from the database but returns a reference to the already-instantiated object. Because another internal session could have already modified the object in the database in the meantime, you would unintentionally overwrite the changes the other internal session made in this case.

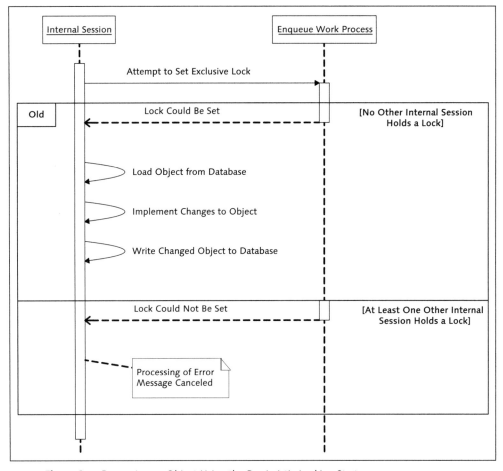

Figure 8.2 Processing an Object Using the Pessimistic Locking Strategy

The exclusive lock is usually automatically removed at the end of the top-level transaction. Only in the Direct Update mode should you explicitly remove the exclusive lock by calling the corresponding lock module if the internal session will continue to be used.

If setting the exclusive lock fails, another internal session already processes the same object. In this case, you must cancel the processing of the object and possibly try at a later point in time to set the lock.

8.2.3 Optimistic Locking

If you pursue the optimistic locking strategy, you don't use the SAP Lock Concept initially to prevent multiple internal sessions from working with the same object. Instead, you use the SAP Lock Concept to determine whether the object you work with has been modified by another internal session since you've loaded it from the database. Only for the short period of time in which you finish the top-level transaction and write modifications to the object into the database, you ensure that no other internal session writes the same object into the database at the same time.

The UML sequence diagram in Figure 8.3 shows the resulting process. Here again, the sequence is important in which you set the lock and load the object from the database: The optimistic lock must be set in any case before you load the object that you want to work with from the database. After you've modified the object in the main memory, you convert the optimistic lock into an exclusive lock. If this step is successful, no other internal session has modified the object in the database since the object has been loaded from the database.

The exclusive lock that is now set ensures that no other internal session writes the same object into the database at the same time. Also, all other internal sessions that had set an optimistic mode for the same object lose their optimistic lock. This way, the other internal sessions are informed that their version of the object is no longer the current version. After the successful conversion, you can write the modifications that you've made to the object into the database.

If the conversion fails, the object has already been processed by another internal session in the meantime. The other internal session has successfully converted its optimistic lock into an exclusive lock; as a result, you've lost your optimistic lock. You must therefore abort the processing and undo the modifications that you have already made to the object. If you try again to process the object, the process starts all over again. You must set an optimistic lock and then ensure that the class agent reloads the object from the database (see Section 3.4, Management States of Persistent Objects, in Chapter 3).

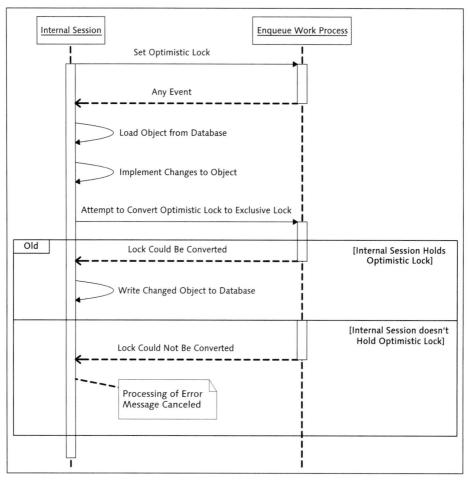

Figure 8.3   Processing an Object Using the Optimistic Locking Strategy

In the optimistic locking strategy, the optimistic lock indicates at any time whether the version of an object that you've loaded from the database is still current: If the optimistic lock is still set, you work with the current status of the object. If the lock is no longer set, another internal session has already modified the object or has at least announced that it will modify the object. The decisive point in time at which the optimistic lock must be available is the point in time when the lock is converted.

In theory, when you set the optimistic lock, you can also check whether you've been able to set the lock successfully, or you can check during the object processing whether the lock is still set. Such an approach, however, contradicts the purely optimistic approach and doesn't result in any important added value. Besides the additional checks, you also have to implement a suitable cancellation of the processing at multiple points, which makes your application considerably more complex and thus more difficult to maintain. In the optimistic locking strategy, it's therefore advisable only to evaluate whether you were able to convert the lock.

By using optimistic locking, you minimize the duration for which an exclusive lock is set for the processed object. You only need to set an exclusive lock for as long as the already-determined changes are written to the database. Particularly in applications that interact with the user after loading the object, you can considerably reduce the time in which the exclusive lock is set. You also only need to lock exclusively if you actually modify the object. If you find out after the object has been loaded that you don't want to write any changes to the database, for example, because the user cancels processing, you don't need any exclusive lock at all. With optimistic locking, you therefore also reduce the number of cases in which you must set an exclusive lock.

8.2.4 Using the Two Locking Strategies in an SAP System

When you use the SAP Lock Concept, you don't need to decide on one of the two presented locking strategies and use it consistently. In an SAP system, you can also work with pessimistic locking in some applications and with optimistic locking in others. Even if applications with different locking strategies work with the same objects, using the SAP Lock Concept you will still attain an effective, reliable protection against inconsistencies caused by concurrent accesses.

If you use the pessimistic locking here as described in Section 8.2.2, Pessimistic Locking, the applications that work with optimistic locking have priority over applications that work with pessimistic locking: As soon as an optimistic lock for an object is set, no other session can directly set an exclusive lock to the same object. Applications that work with pessimistic locking therefore not only need to wait until no other internal session has set an exclusive lock but also until no other internal session has set an optimistic lock.

If required, you can also reverse this priority: For this purpose, in the pessimistic locking strategy, you don't directly set an exclusive lock but initially an optimistic one, which you immediately convert into an exclusive lock. This way, all other internal sessions lose their optimistic lock for the object, and you get an exclusive lock although optimistic locks were set. The only situation in which you can't set an exclusive lock this way is if another internal session already holds an exclusive lock for the object.

8.3   Integration of Optimistic Locking

It's possible to integrate optimistic locking with Object Services through simple enhancements to the persistent classes and your class agents. If you've made the enhancements which are presented in this section to a persistent class and the corresponding class agent, every object of the class automatically ensures the correct use of the optimistic locking strategy. The applications that work with the objects of the persistent class neither need to explicitly set the optimistic lock nor convert the lock.

These enhancements of the class agent ensure that an optimistic lock is always set before a persistent object is loaded, so you don't need to carry out this step manually in the application. Simultaneously, you exclude a frequent source of error because you make sure that the optimistic lock is set always before an object is loaded and never afterwards.

As soon as you make the first modification to a persistent object, the enhanced class agent automatically registers the modified object as a check agent. If you then conclude the transaction, the Transaction Service automatically calls the methods for the consistency check in all persistent objects that you've modified. Within the consistency check, the persistent object ensures that no modified version of the object exists in the database yet and that the object is locked exclusively.

This way, the persistent class and the class agent make sure that you don't write any modifications to a persistent object to the database without using the SAP Lock Concept correctly. Applications that work with the objects of a persistent class that was enhanced this way don't need to take care of setting locks and of adhering to the correct sequence when loading objects.

The applications that work with the objects of a persistent class with the integrated lock concept only need to meet two easy requirements:

▶ The applications themselves must not directly set locks for the persistent objects. All locks that result in an effective implementation of the optimistic locking strategy are set by the persistent class and the class agent automatically. Additional locks are therefore only an unnecessary source of error that may lead to inconsistencies.

▶ When finishing a transaction, the applications should catch exceptions of the `CX_OS_CHECK_AGENT_FAILED` class that occur if the optimistic lock wasn't converted into an exclusive one. If an application doesn't catch such an exception, the automated lock process still prevents inconsistent data from occurring due to concurrent accesses. In this case, a short dump emerges, which is very easy to identify and resolve compared to other errors that arise if you use the SAP Lock Concept in the wrong way.

8.3.1 Setting Optimistic Locks

To implement the optimistic locking strategy, you must set an optimistic lock before the corresponding object is loaded from the database. Before a persistent object is loaded from the database, the object usually doesn't yet exist in the memory. Therefore, an integration of setting the optimistic lock isn't directly possible in the persistent class.

The class agent of the persistent class loads the object from the database. In the class of the class agent, it's therefore possible to integrate setting the locks before loading the object. For example, you can enhance the methods that you call for instantiating a persistent object, such as the `GET_PERSISTENT` method. Because this method returns an already-loaded object when it is repeatedly called with the same key and it doesn't reload the object from the database in this case, you run the risk of setting an optimistic lock after loading the object. Setting an optimistic lock in such a case would result in a gap in the locking strategy. Also, the method isn't run if the class agent sets a persistent object from the `NOT LOADED` management state to the `LOADED` management state, which occurs, for example, after the start of a new top-level transaction or after the call of the `REFRESH_PERSISTENT` method.

You can avoid these disadvantages by enhancing the method that loads the object from the database. For persistent classes, for which a business key is defined in the persistence representation, this is the `MAP_LOAD_FROM_DATABASE_KEY` method. This method is called whenever a persistent object is loaded from the database whose business key is already known, which means it's run both during the instantiation, for instance, via the GET_PERSISTENT method, and in the transition from the NOT LOADED management state to the LOADED management state.

The Persistence Service automatically generates the MAP_LOAD_FROM_DATABASE_KEY method in the class of the base agent. In the class of the class agent, which is a subclass of the base agent's class, you can redefine the method and enhance it with any additional functionality. Listing 8.2 shows how you can enhance the method so that it initially sets an optimistic lock and then reads the required object from the database.

```
METHOD map_load_from_database_key.
  DATA: wa_business_key TYPE typ_business_key.

  LOOP AT i_business_key_tab INTO wa_business_key.
*   Set an optimistic lock for the object to be
*   loaded
    CALL FUNCTION 'ENQUEUE_ESFLIGHT'
      EXPORTING
        mode_sflight   = 'O'
        carrid         = wa_business_key-carrid
        connid         = wa_business_key-connid
        fldate         = wa_business_key-fldate
      EXCEPTIONS
        foreign_lock   = 1
        system_failure = 2
        OTHERS         = 3.
  ENDLOOP.

* Call of the generated method in the superclass
  result =
    super->map_load_from_database_key( i_business_key_tab ).
ENDMETHOD.
```

Listing 8.2 Setting Optimistic Locks Prior to Loading Persistent Objects from the Database

The MAP_LOAD_FROM_DATABASE_KEY method in its original form loads the data for all persistent attributes of the corresponding object from the database for each business key that is passed as an internal table using the I_BUSINESS_KEY_TAB importing parameter. It then uses the RESULT returning parameter to return the result to the caller.

The redefined method calls the lock module for the ESFLIGHT lock object for each individual transferred business key in a LOOP to set an optimistic lock for each corresponding object. The method passes the lock mode '0' and the individual components of the business key to the lock module. The classic exceptions that can be raised when setting the lock are listed in the call. This isn't followed by an evaluation of whether such an exception was raised. As Section 8.2.3, Optimistic Locking, already described, in the optimistic locking strategy, it isn't necessary to evaluate the success of setting the optimistic lock. However, the subsequent evaluation of success for the conversion of the optimistic lock into an exclusive lock is important.

After the optimistic lock has been set for all requested objects, the method calls its equivalent in the superclass. Here, you can find the Open SQL statement that loads the data from the database. The result of the method in the superclass is directly forwarded to the calling program via the RESULT parameter.

Through the redefinition and the call of the generated method in the superclass, the method also adapts after changes to the object-relational mapping, which you make in the persistence representation dialog. You only need to adjust the lock object and the call of the lock module if you change the key of the persistent class.

You can also enhance the class agent of persistent classes whose objects are managed via an instance GUID. For this purpose, you redefine the MAP_LOAD_FROM_DATABASE_GUID method. Instead of the business key, in this case you transfer the instance GUID of an object to be instantiated to the lock module.

> **Warning: Redefining Methods in the Class Agent**
>
> If you redefine a method in the class of a class agent to enhance the functionality of the class agent, you shouldn't exit the method without calling the corresponding method in the superclass. This also applies in cases in which an exception is raised or if you determine that the enhancement you've implemented isn't supposed to be executed. If you leave the method without calling the method in the superclass, you run the risk of leaving the class agent in an inconsistent state.

Number of Locks Set

If you use the optimistic locking strategy, you generate a considerably larger number of entries in the lock table than when you use the pessimistic locking strategy. Usually, you also set optimistic locks for objects that you don't change. The optimistic lock doesn't prevent other internal sessions from working with the object for which you've set an optimistic lock, but the capacity of the lock table is limited.

So, it can make sense to set no optimistic locks for objects in applications that load many objects and access them in read only mode. For example, you could add a Boolean attribute, SET_OPTIMISTIC_LOCKS, to the class agent; this Boolean attribute would notify the class agent of whether it's supposed to set optimistic locks automatically. Provided that you, as described in the following, automatically register changed objects as check agents, such an attribute doesn't bear the risk that you write changes to the database without having set the necessary locks.

You specify the maximum size of the lock table via the enque/table_size profile parameter. If the size of the lock table in your system isn't sufficient to manage the required locks, your SAP system administrator can increase the size of the lock table using this profile parameter.

Setting Optimistic Locks When Using the Query Service

The integration of setting the optimistic lock as shown earlier in Listing 8.2 doesn't apply if you instantiate persistent objects via the Query Service. For setting any lock, it's necessary to already know the key of the object before the object is loaded from the database. The Query Service uses a database query to load objects from the database whose key hasn't been known on the application server before. In this procedure, there's no option to set a lock at the right time.

However, alternative procedures, with which you can set locks even if you use the Query Service, have the result that you can't load objects from the database with only one database access. The biggest advantage of using the Query Service — the reduced runtime — is thus lost. Among others, the following approaches are possible:

▶ You can reload all objects from the database that you've instantiated using the Query Service. For this purpose, you call the IF_OS_FACTORY~REFRESH_PERSIS-TENT method of the class agent. For the next access to the object, the Persistence Service automatically reloads the object from the database and calls the MAP_LOAD_FROM_DATABASE_KEY method or the MAP_LOAD_FROM_DATABASE_GUID method in which you set the optimistic lock.

▸ The Query Service uses the `MAP_LOAD_FROM_DATABASE` method of the class agent to load objects from the database that meet the filter condition. You can redefine this method and first only determine the keys of the objects that correspond to the filter conditions in an initial database query. With these keys, you then call the `MAP_LOAD_FROM_DATABASE_KEY` method or the `MAP_LOAD_FROM_DATABASE_GUID` method that loads the remaining attributes of the objects from the database for the keys determined after it set the optimistic lock.

8.3.2 Registering the Check Agent

You must convert the set optimistic lock into an exclusive lock for all persistent objects that you modify. If the conversion fails, you must not write the modified objects to the database. Object Services provide an option with which you can still cancel the process of writing changes to the database: the consistency checks of check agents. If one of the consistency checks of the registered check agents fails at the end of a transaction, the Transaction Service doesn't write the changes to the database and doesn't end the transaction.

To approach the goal of the optimistic locking strategy to set exclusive locks only for a very short period of time, the conversion of locks should be implemented as late as possible. Because in the context of Object Services, there's hardly any later point in time to integrate the conversion, the mechanism of check agents is used to convert the optimistic locks into exclusive locks.

For this purpose, you must register each changed object as a check agent. Each object then executes the conversion of its own lock before it is written to the database. You could also leave it up to the applications to register each changed object as a check agent. However, this approach is error-prone: If an application doesn't register an application as a check agent, there's no protection against concurrent accesses to this object. Because no exceptions or short dumps would occur, such an error would be difficult to identify. You can eliminate this source of error by registering the changed object automatically as a check agent.

The `HANDLER_CHANGED` method of the class agent is run once for each persistent object when the first change is made to a persistent attribute of the object. You can redefine this method as well to enhance its functionality. Listing 8.3 shows how you can enhance the method so that it registers the changed object at the running top-level transaction as a check agent whenever the method is executed.

```
METHOD handler_changed.
  DATA:
    ri_check_agent         TYPE REF TO if_os_check,
    ri_top_transaction     TYPE REF TO if_os_transaction,
    ri_transaction_manager TYPE REF TO if_os_transaction_manager.

* Call of the general method in the superclass
  super->handler_changed( sender ).

* Typecast: ANY => IF_OS_CHECK
  ri_check_agent ?= sender.

* Determine the current top-level transaction
  ri_transaction_manager =
    cl_os_system=>get_transaction_manager( ).
  ri_top_transaction =
    ri_transaction_manager->get_top_transaction( ).

* Register the changed object as a check agent
  ri_top_transaction->register_check_agent( ri_check_agent ).
ENDMETHOD.
```

Listing 8.3 Registering a Persistent Object as a Check Agent When It Is Transferred Into the CHANGED Management State

In this redefinition, the implementation of the method from the superclass is called already before running the newly added functions. However, the sequence isn't decisive here. It would also be possible to first register the object as a check agent and then call the implementation of the method from the superclass.

The HANDLER_CHANGED method receives a reference to the persistent object that has just been changed via the SENDER importing parameter. A downcast to the check agent interface is required because the importing parameter has the general type ANY. Via the Transaction Manager, the system determines the running top-level transaction to register the changed object as a check agent.

To register the persistent object as a check agent in the top-level transaction as described, the persistent class must implement the IF_OS_CHECK check agent interface. Also, a top-level transaction must already run. This is another reason why you should create and start the first transaction upon the start of the application; that is, immediately after setting the transaction mode, if you use the object-oriented transaction mode.

By registering the object as a check agent for the top-level transaction, you minimize the time for which an exclusive lock is set. In this case, the error handling
needs to be carried out only once centrally at the end of the top-level transaction. If
the structure of your application doesn't allow for an error handling at the top level,
for instance, because your application runs in the compatibility mode, you can also
register the changed object as a check agent for a running subtransaction.

Altogether, the error handling becomes more tedious through registration of check
agents for subtransactions because you must implement the exception handling
wherever you finish a subtransaction. Moreover you restrict the parallel processing
in the system more strongly than with the registration for the top-level transaction because the exclusive lock is set earlier and therefore remains set for a longer
period of time. For these reasons, you should prefer the registration for the top-
level transaction if possible.

Similar enhancements to the ones presented here are also possible to register persistent objects as check agents during creation or deletion. This way, you can also
use the optimistic locking strategy to protect the database accesses, which write
changed persistent objects to the database or delete persistent objects from there,
against inconsistencies caused by concurrent access.

8.3.3 Converting Optimistic Locks Into Exclusive Locks

After you've automated the setting of the optimistic lock before loading the persistent object and the registration of each changed object as a check agent, you
must carry out a consistency check to convert the optimistic lock into an exclusive lock. For this purpose, the persistent class must implement the IF_OS_CHECK
interface which defines the IS_CONSISTENT method. If you can make sure that only
objects for which Object Services are supposed to write changes to the database
at the end of the top-level transaction are registered as check agents exactly once,
the conversion of the lock will be the only action that you have to perform in the
IS_CONSISTENT method.

Check Agent Actions

For the suggested option to register objects automatically as the check agent, an
object might be registered as a check agent for which no changes are written to
the database at the end. This occurs if you modify an object in a subtransaction,
and you reset the subtransaction using the UNDO method. The object is no longer

modified afterward and isn't written to the database at the end of the top-level transaction. A conversion of the lock isn't required in such cases. Before you convert the lock, you should thus check whether the object is in a management state in which the conversion of the lock is required.

Also, an object might be registered as a check agent multiple times in a transaction. The implementation of the transactions in the CL_OS_TRANSACTION class doesn't check whether an object has already been registered as a check agent before, and it performs the same consistency check multiple times if you register the same object as a check agent multiple times. If you register objects as check agents in the HAN- DLER_CHANGED method as suggested, you might register the same object as a check agent multiple times in the running top-level transaction. When you change an object in a subtransaction, the object is automatically registered as a check agent. If you reset the subtransaction using the UNDO method and then modify the object in the same top-level transaction, the object returns to the CHANGED management state and is re-registered as a check agent by the HANDLER_CHANGED method.

Because the Transaction Service calls the IS_CONSISTENT method of the same object multiple times in such a case, the conversion is only successful in the first run. In the second run, the lock is already converted, and the attempt to convert it again fails. Because the successful conversion in the first run already ensures that no concurrent access to the object occurs when writing to the database, the failed conversion for the repeated call of the method should not have the result that you abort finishing the transaction.

To return the desired result in the two scenarios described, the suggestion for an implementation of the IS_CONSISTENT method includes two further checks in addition to the lock conversion. Figure 8.4 shows the entire process. Before you try to convert the lock, you should first check the management state of the object. Object Services write changes to the database in the CHANGED, NEW, and DELETED management states. In this case, you should continue with the conversion of the lock. If the object is in another management state, no write access to the database occurs. In this case, you don't need to perform any conversion of the lock, and you immediately know that the object is in a consistent state with regard to the optimistic locking strategy.

If the lock conversion was successful, you can safely write the changes to the object into the database. If the conversion failed, you must differentiate two cases: Either the conversion failed because another internal session has changed the same object in the meantime, or the consistency check has been called multiple times and the lock has already been converted successfully in the previous run.

To differentiate the two options, you can determine whether the internal session already holds an exclusive lock for the object. If your internal session doesn't hold any exclusive lock, it's definite that you have to abort the writing of changes to the database. If your internal session already holds an exclusive lock, you can continue with writing changes to the database.

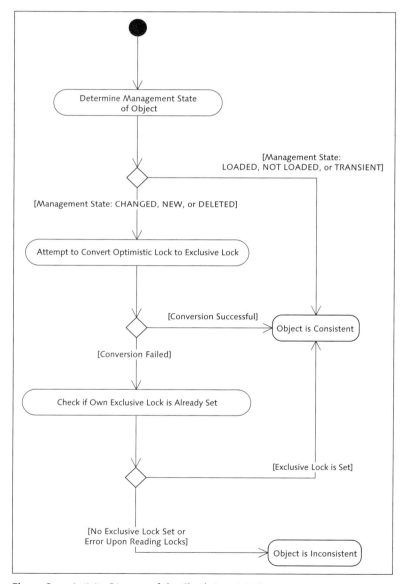

Figure 8.4 Activity Diagram of the Check Agent Actions

Check Agent Implementation

Listing 8.4 shows the ABAP source code for the actions shown in Figure 8.4. The system calls the IF_OS_CA_INSTANCE~GET_STATUS method of the class agent to determine the management state of the object. The result is checked against the constants for the individual management states from the OSCON type group. If an exception is raised when the lock module is called, the lock could not be converted. If no exception is raised, the conversion was successful.

```
METHOD if_os_check~is_consistent.
  DATA: rf_ca_sflight TYPE REF TO /iot/ca_sflight,
        st_buskey     TYPE scol_flight_key,
        v_status      TYPE os_ostatus,
        v_buskey      TYPE eqegraarg.

* Determine the management state of the object
  rf_ca_sflight = /iot/ca_sflight=>agent.
  v_status =
    rf_ca_sflight->if_os_ca_instance~get_status( me ).

* The persistent object was only changed in the
* CHANGED, DELETED, and NEW management states
* End processing for other management states
  IF v_status <> oscon_ostatus_changed AND
     v_status <> oscon_ostatus_deleted AND
     v_status <> oscon_ostatus_new.
*   Object is consistent
    result = abap_true.
    RETURN.
  ENDIF.

* Fill business key from attributes of the objects
  st_buskey-carrid = me->get_carrid( ).
  st_buskey-connid = me->get_connid( ).
  st_buskey-fldate = me->get_fldate( ).

* Try to convert the optimistic lock into an exclusive
* lock
  CALL FUNCTION 'ENQUEUE_ESFLIGHT'
    EXPORTING
      mode_sflight = 'R'
      carrid       = st_buskey-carrid
      connid       = st_buskey-connid
```

```
      fldate          = st_buskey-fldate
    EXCEPTIONS
      foreign_lock    = 1
      system_failure  = 2
      OTHERS          = 3.
  IF sy-subrc = 0.
* Lock could not be converted successfully
* -> End processing, object is consistent
    result = abap_true.
    RETURN.
  ENDIF.


* Lock could not be converted
* Check whether object is already locked exclusively
* by the current internal session
  v_buskey = st_buskey.
  CALL FUNCTION '/IOT/ENQUEUE_CHECK'
    EXPORTING
      im_table_name = 'SFLIGHT'
      im_buskey     = v_buskey
      im_enqmode    = 'E'
    IMPORTING
      ex_exists     = result
    EXCEPTIONS
      error         = 1
      OTHERS        = 2.

  IF sy-subrc <> 0.
* Check for set exclusive lock could not be
* executed
* -> End processing, object is not consistent
    result = abap_false.
    RETURN.
  ENDIF.


ENDMETHOD.
```

Listing 8.4 Converting the Optimistic Lock into an Exclusive Lock Within the Consistency Check

The /IOT/ENQUEUE_CHECK function module is used to check whether the running internal session already holds an exclusive lock. This function module browses the result of the ENQUEUE_READ SAP function module, which returns the locks of all internal sessions for an object, for a lock that the running internal session holds. The returning parameter of the method called RESULT is set to abap_true if the changes may be written to the database; otherwise, it's set to abap_false.

As soon as a check agent returns abap_false as the result while a transaction calls its check agents, the Transaction Service doesn't perform any further consistency checks. With an exception of the CX_OS_CHECK_AGENT_FAILED class, the calling program, which wanted to finish the transaction, is informed that a consistency check failed and that the changes were not written to the database for this reason.

8.4 Integration of Pessimistic Locking

To implement the pessimistic locking strategy in its pure form, it's necessary to set an exclusive lock before the class agent loads an object from the database. Unlike for the optimistic locking strategy, it isn't recommended to fully automate pessimistic locking. A full automation results in locking all objects exclusively that a user currently views. This restricts the parallel working in the system too much because two users can't even look at the same objects at the same time.

An integration of the pessimistic locking strategy should therefore provide the options for applications to decide which objects are locked exclusively and when. Two alternative approaches provide useful options to integrate pessimistic locking with Object Services:

▸ You provide an additional method in the class agent, for instance, a method called LOCK_AND_GET_PERSISTENT. This method sets an exclusive lock for a transferred key and then loads the corresponding object from the database. Here it's important to check whether the object is actually read from the database before you set the lock. You must not set an exclusive lock if the method then returns a reference to an already instantiated object. The method should respond with an exception if setting the exclusive lock fails or if the object for the transferred key is already instantiated.

▸ You provide an additional method in the persistent class, for instance, a method called LOCK. This method ensures that an exclusive lock is set. The process is similar to the implementation of the check agent for optimistic locking described in Section 8.3.3, Converting Optimistic Locks Into Exclusive Locks. Only the check for the management state isn't required in this case. The method initially tries to perform a conversion of the lock. If this fails, it checks whether the running internal session already holds an exclusive lock. It uses a Boolean return value to inform the calling program whether a lock is set or not.

It's important that the method performs a conversion of the lock and doesn't directly set an exclusive lock because the persistent object is usually loaded already. You must not set a lock after loading the corresponding object. You can only set an exclusive lock directly in the NOT LOADED management state. The conversion doesn't result in a pure pessimistic locking strategy: You set the exclusive lock after the object is loaded from the database, and you use an optimistic lock. The result of this approach is very similar to the pessimistic locking strategy because the exclusive lock is already set when you start working with the object. This way, you can ensure in an application that the changes to the objects don't need to be undone retroactively due to a failed conversion of a lock.

Additionally, you possibly need an option to remove an exclusive lock manually. At the end of the top-level transaction, the system removes the lock again; however, if you don't want to exclusively lock an object any longer that is already locked exclusively and that won't be written to the database, a method for removing the exclusive lock should be available in the persistent class.

For both approaches, the application must decide explicitly when it makes sense to lock an object exclusively. For example, this can be the case when the user switches to the change mode. Compared to the direct call of a lock module, the handling for the application is more convenient because it doesn't have to compose the parameters for the call of the lock module.

Also, you achieve additional security because you exclude a frequent source of error: If the application sets the exclusive lock only via one of the described approaches, this ensures the correct sequence for setting the lock and loading the object. This sequence can't be changed due to an erroneous handling.

8.5   Integration of Both Locking Strategies

The pessimistic locking strategy in the described form assumes that the applications use the provided options correctly. For each object that you change, you must set an exclusive lock. If an application changes an object without setting the exclusive lock, this impends concurrent accesses and resulting inconsistencies.

You can achieve considerably increased protection against the erroneous handling by the application for the pessimistic locking strategy by integrating the enhancements for the optimistic locking strategy, which were described in Section 8.3, Integration of the Optimistic Locking. Then the application can explicitly decide to use pessimistic locking for an object by setting an exclusive lock via the class agent or via the persistent class.

For this object, you don't have the risk that the user will make inputs that can't be saved later because the same object had been modified in another internal session. At the same time, it's ensured that the application never writes an object to the database without using the SAP Lock Concept: If the application doesn't set an exclusive lock, optimistic locking is automatically used. If the application changes an object without having it locked exclusively, the conversion of the lock is automatically performed at the end of the transaction.

You can remedy the greatest weakness of the SAP Lock Concept — it's only effective if all applications use it explicitly — by using the described enhancements for all applications that work with Object Services. You require only one functioning implementation of the locking strategies within Object Services and not a new functioning implementation of the locking strategies for each individual application.

You also remove sources of error such as setting a lock after reading from the database or setting a lock even though the object is returned from the management of the class agent and not loaded from the database. The inconsistencies resulting from these errors, which are difficult to identify and are caused by concurrent accesses to an object, no longer occur. The only prerequisite is that the applications only use the methods presented and don't call a lock module directly.

You can decide from an ergonomic perspective which of the locking strategies you ultimately want to select because both locking strategies can be implemented with the same comparably low effort. If a user must make many inputs meticulously before the changes are written to the database, the optimistic locking strategy isn't the best choice. In case of a lock conflict, the user would be informed only at the end that the processed object has been changed in the meantime and that he needs to repeat all inputs. In such a case, the application should set an exclusive lock before the user starts to make inputs; a pessimistic approach is the correct choice here.

For less complex inputs, the disadvantages in the ergonomics area outweigh for the pessimistic locking strategy: As long as a user accesses an object in change mode, no other user can work with the object. This is particularly a problem if a user keeps his session open during his lunch break or even leaves work without ending the session. The object he works with remains blocked until the session is ended. Therefore, optimistic locking is better suited for applications in which the user usually only makes a few inputs before he saves the changes.

8.6 Summary

This chapter described how you integrate the SAP Lock Concept with a persistent class. The integration presented enables the automatic use of the SAP Lock Concept both with the pessimistic locking strategy and with the optimistic locking strategy. This way, you can ensure that the SAP Lock Concept is always used for changes to the objects of the persistent class. At the same time, you prevent the SAP Lock Concept from being used incorrectly. This way, you can completely exclude errors from concurrent accesses that are difficult to identify as the source of error for your applications.

9   Conclusion

Unfortunately, software developers frequently tend to only use services that they've developed themselves. Software developers who have seen and understood how Object Services facilitate the development of software could certainly come to the conclusion that instead of using Object Services, they could implement their own service, which provides similar functions.

In fact, Object Services do not provide additional functions that could not be implemented in ABAP without Object Services. However, there's hardly any reason that justifies the high amount of effort for the development of an additional service that delivers the same functions as Object Services. Like most of the products by SAP, Object Services have an essential advantage: The offered functions meet the majority of the requirements that potential Object Services users have for a service that provides support for object-relational mapping. You can use the existing functions without having to develop one line of ABAP source code for object-relational mapping.

Where the provided functions aren't sufficient, there are numerous options to enhance the individual parts of Object Services accordingly. It would speak against Object Services if it wasn't possible to enhance Object Services with specific functions that could be easily integrated with a custom implementation without Object Services. However, up to today, this kind of situation has never occurred to us, although we have used Object Services to a large extent for several years now.

The examples for which this book described how you can achieve your goal without a great deal of effort despite existing obstacles show the potential for enhancements and improvements Object Services still provide.

You saw how to easily pass data from a persistent object to a structure to display the data in the user interface. It would be much more convenient if you could directly assign persistent objects to an user interface element. In this case, you only had to select which attribute of the object is supposed to be displayed in what form.

The database selection using the Query Service has the advantage that it requires merely one database query. Consequently, it places less load on the database system and ensures that your applications run faster. However, there are still a lot of situations in which you can't use the Query Service and have to work with queries with Open SQL instead.

One of the reasons for this is that you can't formulate more complex filter conditions, such as subqueries and joins, with the Query Service. Also the approach of directly loading the objects from a database using a single database query for any filter condition doesn't provide the option to set locks before loading the objects because the object keys are usually not known. Also, it does seem to make sense to have the Query Service automatically consider recently created or changed persistent objects in the memory. This book also discussed how you can manually enhance your application accordingly. A similar approach could be used for the integration with Object Services.

Only a few applications in SAP NetWeaver AS ABAP are written for being used by only one user, so it's necessary in nearly all applications to integrate the SAP Lock Concept. You learned how to integrate the SAP Lock Concept into the persistent classes and the corresponding class agents with reasonable effort. The resulting increase of reliability for your applications is significant because there's hardly the risk that concurrent database accesses are inadvertently implemented due to an incorrect use of the SAP Lock Concept.

If SAP already delivered Object Services with a comparable integration of the SAP Lock Concept, the implementation effort would be further reduced for all Object Services users. On top of that, the automated lock procedures for all current users of classic ABAP and of custom developments for object-relational mapping would provide an additional incentive for using Object Services in the future.

Even without additional enhancements by SAP, the use of Object Services in their current form already provides added value to the development of information systems. This added value is further increased if you enhance Object Services with additional functions as described in this book.

We hope that after reading this book, you're convinced by the benefits the software development with Object Services offers you and that you look forward to using Object Services for your future development projects.

The Authors

Christian Assig studied informatics at the University of Applied Sciences of Gelsenkirchen, Germany, and at the University of Western Australia in Perth, Australia. Since 2004, he has worked at IOT (Institut für Organisations- und Technikgestaltung GmbH) providing his support mainly for setting up object-oriented frameworks with ABAP Objects. He makes major contributions to the enterprise-wide establishment of object-oriented models and language elements in the development of information systems in ABAP.

Aldo Hermann Fobbe studied informatics at the University of Applied Sciences of Gelsenkirchen, Germany. Since 2000, he has worked at IOT (Institut für Organisations- und Technikgestaltung GmbH) as a manager for product development and technology in the SAP NetWeaver environment. He contributed to the development of an ABAP Objects-based manufacturing execution system by setting the course for a service-oriented software architecture based on SAP NetWeaver Application Server ABAP at an early stage.

Prof. Dr. Arno Niemietz studied physics and mathematics at the Westphalian Wilhelm University of Münster, Germany. After he received his PhD, he worked for various enterprises in the area of software development. Since 1987, his work has focused on business information systems. In 1990, he was appointed to a professorship at the University of Applied Sciences of Gelsenkirchen, Germany. He teaches in the informatics department and researches in the area of business information systems. In 1998, he founded IOT Institut für Organisations- und Technikgestaltung GmbH (Institute for Organization and Technology Design), which develops business solutions based on SAP technologies.

Index

The definitive SAP rules for ABAP development

Detailed examples of good and poor programming style

With numerous recommendations for everyday programming

Horst Keller, Wolf Hagen Thümmel

Official ABAP Programming Guidelines

How do you program good ABAP? This book, the official SAP programming style guide, will show you how to maximize performance, readability, and stability in your ABAP programs. Sorted by programming tasks, this book will provide you with guidelines on how to best fulfill each task. Starting with basic considerations about the use of comprehensive programming concepts, the book continues with formal criteria such as organizing your source code, and then concludes with descriptions of the various areas and tasks of ABAP development. Filled with real-life code examples, both good and bad, this book is a must-have guide for ABAP developers.

398 pp., 69,95 Euro / US$ 69.95
ISBN 978-1-59229-290-5

>> www.sap-press.com

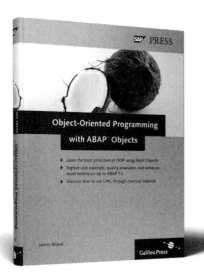

Learn the basic principles of OOP using ABAP Objects

Explore core concepts, quality assurance and enhancement techniques up to ABAP 7.0

Discover how to use UML through practical tutorials

James Wood

Object-Oriented Programming with ABAP Objects

This book provides a gentle (and yet, comprehensive) start to programming object-oriented ABAP! What are objects? How to define and write classes? What's polymorphism all about? The book helps you to venture the switch to object-oriented programming, and brings your skills up to date: First learn about all essential OO concepts, then see examples from daily development work. Exception handling, object debugging and unit testing are demystified here, plus, you get advice on enhanced techniques and tools in ABAP 7.0.

357 pp., 2009, 69,95 Euro / US$ 69.95
ISBN 978-1-59229-235-6

>> www.sap-press.com

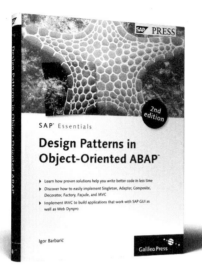

Get a detailed introduction to the
concept of Design Patterns

Learn how to easily implement
Singleton, Adapter, Composite,
Decorator, Factory, Façade, and MVC

Including MVC implementation for
Web Dynpro ABAP

Igor Barbaric

Design Patterns in Object-Oriented ABAP

Design patterns provide you with proven solutions for everyday coding
problems. This SAP PRESS Essentials guide shows how to apply them to
your favourite language: ABAP. Expanded by the implementation of the
MVC pattern in Web Dynpro and a new chapter on the Factory pattern,
this second edition of our programming workshop now covers all
important patterns and all up-to-date ABAP techniques. Watch how the
expert codes the patterns and immediately benefit from better stability
and maintainability of your code!

254 pp., 2. edition, 69,95 Euro / US$ 84.95
ISBN 978-1-59229-263-9

>> www.sap-press.com

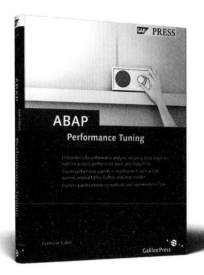

Tools for performance analysis: Code Inspector, runtime analysis, performance trace, and more

Performance aspects in development: SQL queries, internal tables, buffer, data transfer

Application design: general performance and parallelization

Hermann Gahm

ABAP Performance Tuning

This book for ABAP developers details best practices for ABAP performance tuning. Covering the most critical performance-relevant programming issues and performance monitoring tools, this book will show you how to best analyze, tune, and implement your ABAP programs.
Starting with a description of the client/server architecture, the book moves on to discussing the different tools for analyzing performance. Programming techniques are then analyzed in detail, based on numerous real-life examples. This book will help you ensure that your ABAP programs are tuned for best performance.

348 pp., 2009, 69,95 Euro / US$ 69.95
ISBN 978-1-59229-289-9

>> www.sap-press.com

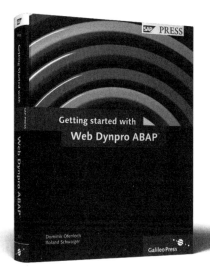

Explains architecture, basic principles, and real-life solutions

Provides step-by-step guidance on the first functional Web Dynpro application

Covers UI elements, standard components, and dynamic applications

Dominik Ofenloch, Roland Schwaiger

Getting Started with Web Dynpro ABAP

Web Dynpro ABAP is the standard UI technology used by SAP for the development of web applications on SAP NetWeaver Application Server ABAP. This book makes it easier for developers with existing ABAP knowledge to become familiar with the component-based UI development environment, and lays the foundation for the creation of complex applications based on Web Dynpro ABAP. It discusses the functions and special features that are critical for you if you're a beginner, and is structured so that you can understand basic concepts and see real-life examples. This is the one resource you need to get up to speed with Web Dynpro ABAP.

477 pp., 2010, 69,95 Euro / US$ 69.95
ISBN 978-1-59229-311-7

>> **www.sap-press.com**

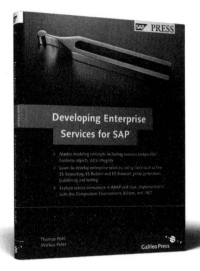

Modeling: Services meta model, enterprise services repository, ARIS

Development: proxy generation, inbound services, synchronous and asynchronous communication

Usage: consumer proxies in ABAP and Java, security, error handling

Thomas Pohl, Markus Peter

Developing Enterprise Services for SAP

This book is a developer's guide to programming enterprise services. After reading this book, you will be able to develop enterprise services in ABAP and in Java, and you'll then be able to integrate these services into larger applications.
You will be guided through the modeling process, the development of services, and finally to the implementation of the service. Using numerous screenshots of the Workbench and Eclipse, and showing numerous code listings, this book will help you understand how to develop enterprise services.

396 pp., 2009, 69,95 Euro / US$ 69.95
ISBN 978-1-59229-291-2

>> **www.sap-press.com**